University of Nebraska Press
Lincoln and London

The Modern Cowboy

The Modern Cowboy

JOHN R. ERICKSON

Photographs by Kris Erickson

Portions of this book have appeared in the following publications in slightly different form, and are used with permission: Chapter 5, "Cowboy Vices and Recreation," in the "Scene" magazine of the *Dallas Morning News,* March 4, 1979, pp. 14–16; Chapter 8, "Pickups and Trailers," in the *Livestock Weekly,* October 26, 1978, pp. 10, 11; and Chapter 9, "Pasture Roping, Then and Now," in the *Cattleman,* October and November 1979, pp. 48–56 and pp. 100–102, 106–8, respectively.

Library of Congress Cataloging in Publication Data

Erickson, John R   1943–
  The modern cowboy.

  Bibliography: p.
  1. Cowboys—The West.   2. The West—Social life and customs.   I. Title.
F596.E74   636.2'13   80–28751
ISBN 0–8032–1805–2

To my mother-in-law, Mary Dykema

Contents

Illustrations

Author's Note

It is almost impossible to make a general statement about cowboys or ranching without getting into an argument with someone. It seems that everyone involved in the cattle business has his own way of doing things.

Cowboying in the Texas Panhandle is not exactly the same as cowboying in California; it's not even the same as cowboying in East Texas. Differences among cowboys arise from several factors: history, tradition, weather, and terrain, to name a few. Wherever they live, cowboys figure out their own solutions to their own particular set of problems and adapt their tools and techniques to the situations they face. And of course, being cowboys, they will add a little something of their own, out of sheer orneriness if they can't find a better reason.

The perfect book on modern cowboying would deal with cowboys in all parts of the country, from the Texas Gulf coast to the mountains of Montana, from Florida to Oregon. It would describe cowboys of the swamp, forest, mountains, desert, brush, coast, and plains.

This is not the perfect book. I am writing out of my own experience as a working cowboy in the Texas and Oklahoma panhandles. I have never followed a chuckwagon on a giant ranch, roped horses out of a remuda, chased cattle down a mountain slope, or worked cowdogs in heavy brush.

There are a lot of things I haven't done and don't know.

There is no disgrace in this, because you can't possibly know everything about everything. The only disgrace would come in trying to convince a trusting reader that you did, or thought you did. In the following pages, when I dare to make general statements and say, ''Cowboys do this,'' or, ''Cowboys think that,'' the reader should be aware that I am speaking of cowboys I have known in places where I have lived and worked, and that another writer in another part of the country might see his subject somewhat differently.

PART ONE: THE MODERN COWBOY

1

What Is a Cowboy?

In 1978 and 1979 I was working as a cowboy on a ranch in Beaver County, Oklahoma. In the depths of January, I drove over to the next ranch and found my good friend and cowboy companion, Jake Parker. "Jake," I said, "we're about to starve out. We just can't make it on six hundred dollars a month. Inflation is killing us and I'm so danged tired of feeding cattle seven days a week that I could scream." Jake nodded.

In February I caught Jake as he was coming in from his feed run. "Jake," I said, "we're just barely getting by. If everyone stays healthy and the car doesn't break down, we'll make it. But if something goes wrong . . . I guess I'd better start looking around for another line of work."

Jake nodded. He understood.

In March I helped Jake do some cattle work. It was the first time we had been a-horseback since January. The day was warm and most of the snow had melted off the sandhills. Our horses felt good and so did we. "Parker," I said, "I'm looking forward to spring roundup season, aren't you?" He smiled and said, "You bet."

In April we were riding on a roundup crew, laughing and joking with the other cowboys, drinking in the spring air, working our horses, and playing with our ropes. And I said, "You know, Parker, we're damned lucky that

Cowboy work is more than a job; it is a life-style and a medium of expression.

3

Jake Parker of the Three Cross Ranch in Beaver County, Oklahoma, and Buck, his big quarter horse, ready to rope and doctor a sick animal on wheat pasture. Jake has taken his reins out of the martingale, which hangs from the breast strap because he doesn't want it pulling on Buck's head when the chase begins. The martingale is used to "set" a horse's head, so that he holds it at the proper angle.

somebody will pay us money for doing this." Jake laughed and said, "Yalp."

I have met the American cowboy on ranches in the Texas and Oklahoma Panhandles. I have ridden with him and worked beside him. I have eaten lunch with him on the ground and drunk water from his cup. I am tempted to describe him as I have seen him described in several books: "Merely folks, just a plain everyday bowlegged human." It is a marvelous description, and very quotable. However, the temptation to use it merely points out the degree to which, on the subject of cowboys, we have come to rely on books and observations of the past. The fact is—and I rather hate to admit this—that I have known only one bowlegged cowboy, and I think he was born that way. Legend tells us that cowboys are supposed to have legs warped by long days in the saddle, and maybe fifty years ago they did. Today they don't. We can begin our description of the modern cowboy with the observation that, at least on one point of anatomy, he ain't what he used to be.

The cowboy I know is a workingman. He is defined by his work, which should not be confused with the term "job." Cowboy work is more than a job; it is a life-style and a medium of expression. Remove the cowboy from his working environment and you have someone else, someone who resembles a cowboy in outward appearance but who, to one degree or another, is an imposter. Standing on a street corner, the cowboy is just an ordinary human. But out in the pasture, when he's a-horseback and holds a rope in his hands, he assumes the qualities that have made him a legend.

The fact that the cowboy is defined by his work has made him a difficult subject to study. To see him at his best, you almost have to work with him day after day, and to understand what he does in his work, you almost have to possess a fundamental knowledge of the skills of his profession. Perhaps the people who are in the best position to observe and discuss the working cowboy are the men who work with him every day—other cowboys. Unfortunately, most cowboys don't write, and most writers don't work on ranches.

The cowboy does not own property. Owners of ranchland go by various titles, among them rancher, cattleman, and stockman. The rancher owns the land, manages the operation, and makes decisions about buying and selling. Of course you can find instances where the two roles overlap. Some ranchers work beside their cowboys, and some cowboys are permitted to make management decisions, and in small ranching operations family members function in both capacities. But as a general rule it is safe to say that ranchers and cowboys are not the same breed. The term *cowboy*, as I use it, means a workingman who has mastered the skills needed in working around cattle, while the term *rancher* implies ownership and management.

In the cow lot or on a roundup crew the social differences between rancher and cowboy don't mean much, but elsewhere they are clearly defined. Ranchers are often prominent leaders in the community; cowboys are not. Ranchers often sit on governing boards of businesses, churches, and schools; cowboys do not. Ranchers are frequently the subject of articles in livestock journals, while the cowboys are rarely mentioned. The rancher and his wife may belong to the country club, but the cowboy and his wife won't. The rancher has his circle of friends, the cowboy has his, and they do not often overlap.

There is one difference between them that goes right to the heart of the matter: the rancher can take the day off or go into town whenever he wishes, but the cowboy can't. The cowboy's life is tied to the rhythms and patterns of animals: a cow that must be milked twice a day, chickens that must be

The weathered face of a cowboy, a common laborer with heroic tendencies and a sense of humor.

turned out in the morning and shut up at night, horses that must be fed and watered, pregnant heifers that must be watched, and, in winter, cows that must be fed seven days a week. The rancher and the cowboy may dress alike, talk alike, and even think alike, but at six o'clock in the evening, one goes down to the milking barn while the other attends a meeting in town.

The cowboy is a workingman, yet he has little in common with the urban blue-collar worker. In the first place, as we have already observed, cowboy work is not just a job, with established work days, certain hours, and guaranteed holidays. Since he lives where he works, and since he deals with animals instead of machines, the cowboy is never really off work. He is on call 24 hours a day, 7 days a week, 365 days a year. The work is not always hard, but as a friend once observed to me, "It's damned sure steady." A calving heifer, a prairie fire, a sick horse may have him up at any hour of the day or night, and in this business there is no such thing as time-and-a-half for overtime.

In the second place, cowboys, unlike urban blue-collar workers, do not belong to a union, and they probably never will. The cowboy life attracts a special type of individual, one who can shift for himself and endure isolation, and one who thrives on physical hardship, a certain amount of danger, and low wages. These are not the qualities of a joiner, but of a loner. You might even go so far as to say that there is a little bit of outlaw in most of them—not that they are dishonest or deceitful, but rather that they are incorrigible, like a spirited horse that is never quite broke and gentle, even though he may take the bit and saddle. Some cowboys stay in the profession simply because they don't fit anywhere else. They tried other jobs and couldn't adapt, or they went into business for themselves and failed. They returned to cowboying because it was in their bones and blood.

This stubborn, independent quality of the cowboy has fascinated the American public and has contributed to his status as a myth and a legend. We like to think of ourselves as a free and independent people, ready at any moment to tell the boss, the mayor, or the president himself to go straight to hell. Of course this is more a dream than a reality. Most of us are indentured to mortgage payments and car payments and live in terror of an IRS audit. Perhaps the cowboy, riding his horse across an endless prairie, has become a symbol of what we used to be—or at least what we *think* we used to be—and of what we would be if we could. He doesn't have to punch a time clock, drive through snarls of traffic every morning and afternoon, shave or wear a tie to work, or participate in hollow rituals in order to gain advancement. When he gets tired of the scenery, or if the boss crowds him too close, he packs his few possessions in a pickup and horse trailer and moves on to another ranch. In the American cowboy we find qualities we deeply admire—simplicity, independence, physical strength, courage, peace of mind, and self-respect—but which, to one degree or another, we have surrendered in order to gain something else. These qualities have made the cowboy the most powerful mythical character in our folklore, and one which reaches to the very core of our identity as a people.

The typical cowboy, if we may speak of such an animal, does not carry a pistol, strum a guitar, or burst into song at the end of the day. He has never rescued a maiden in distress or cleaned the outlaws out of a saloon. He can ride a bucking horse, but he can also get piled. He can rope a calf in the pasture, but he can also burn three loops before he makes the catch. In his working environment, he is dressed in blue jeans, a long-sleeved shirt, boots, western hat, and a vest. He looks good in these clothes, like an animal in its skin. In his work he moves with ease and grace, and sitting astride his horse he exudes confidence and authority. We are tempted to say that he is handsome, even though he might lack the physical endowments that we usually associate with that term.

But take him off his horse, throw him into a bathtub, scrub him down, put him in a set of "good" clothes, and send him to town, and we will meet an entirely different man. All at once he becomes graceless and awkward. He isn't wearing his work hat and we see that he is getting bald, or if he has a good head of hair, it looks as though he has plastered it with lard and run a rake through it. His eyes, which outside are naturally set into a squint, seem puffy in the fluorescent light, and they do not sparkle. His "good" clothes are appalling, and we can hardly keep from laughing at him.

The mythology and legend of the Cowboy begin in this humble human vessel. But the working cowboy is neither a myth nor a legend. He is an ordinary mortal. If we stopped at this point, we would have performed the ritual known as debunking, wherein a notable figure is taken like a buck deer, strung up, skinned and gutted, and held up naked for all to see. But I'm not setting out to debunk the cowboy. If he sometimes falls short of our expectations, he will surpass them when we see him at his best. And he is at his best when he is at his work. Ultimately, the cowboy *is* what he *does*.

So what is a cowboy? Is he a heroic figure or just a common laborer? It's hard to say. I've seen both sides, and I think it would be a mistake to place too much emphasis on one side or the other. If we view him only as a symbol and a mythical figure, then we lose contact with his humanness and fall into the kind of sentimentality that allows some observers to ignore the poverty, the loneliness, the exploitation of cowboys, and to gloss over the darker side of the cattle industry with little homilies about the "honor" of being a cowboy. But neither do we want to strip him down to enzymes and electrons or to present him as just another human fop doomed to mediocrity and failure, for this view would deny that he can rise above himself through displays of skill, strength, and courage. And that would be false.

If the cowboy is a hero, then we will want to know the price he pays for this honor. If he is a common man, then we will want to know why he has fascinated our people for a hundred years. For the moment let us content ourselves with this definition: The cowboy is a common laborer with heroic tendencies and a sense of humor.

2

What He Looks Like, What He Wears

Cowboy dress is determined by three factors: weather, work, and vanity.

The cowboys I have known were pretty much average-sized fellows, rarely very tall, very short, or very fat. The shortest man I ever worked with stood about five foot seven, while the tallest, Jim Gregg of Beaver, Oklahoma, was six foot six. (Jim came from a family of big men. His great-uncle Hugh McFarland ranched along the Beaver River, rode horseback all his life, and was regarded as a top hand. At six foot nine, he may have been one of America's tallest horsemen.) The stoutest cowboys I've known weighed about 215 or 220 pounds. But most fell into the range of average height and weight, standing between five foot ten and six foot two and weighing from 150 to 200 pounds.

Perhaps this physical description fits a national average and would be the same in other professions and trades, but I suspect there is more to it than that. If you observe people in a public place, such as an airport or a bus station, you will notice that there are a lot of tall and short men in this world. If you observe physical shapes in a restaurant, you might be surprised at how many of our countrymen are porky. Yet, on a roundup crew composed of full-time cowboys, you do not see these extremes of physical types, which makes me think that there is something in the nature of the work that repels the very short, the very tall, and the overweight. Maybe fat men lack the endurance for heavy physical work or the ability to perform in extreme heat.

There is also the possibility that, under the rigors of the profession, fat men tend to become unfat and to remain that way.

The typical cowboy, as I have observed him, may have a paunch and a little weatherboarding around his middle, but he isn't fat, and more often than not, he is thin, wiry, and trim at the waist. He has quick reflexes, good endurance, and strong hands, arms, and shoulders. Upper body strength is important in this business, since many of the routine jobs on a ranch demand it: digging postholes, pulling the rods out of a windmill, lifting bales of hay and sacks of feed, holding calves down in a branding pen, and wrestling with iron-jawed horses. The cowboy may not have the build of a weight lifter or a football player, but what flesh he carries is hard and tough. Like the jackrabbit, he wouldn't be fit to eat.

A cowboy's hands tell the story of his work. You rarely see one with delicate hands, the kind a piano player might be proud of. Most often the fingers are thickened by constant use, the palms rough enough to snag on delicate fabrics, the top side scarred and scabbed, and the nails bearing evidence of abuse.

Whether a cowboy has a lantern jaw or a chin like Slim Pickens, buck teeth or no teeth at all, a thick head of hair or nothing but imagination to run a comb through, his face will often have a weathered look by the time he turns forty. Cowboys are exposed to wind and the constant glare of the sun, and to protect their eyes they squint. Over a period of years their eyes begin to narrow, and wrinkles and creases form in the corner. If cowboys survive long enough as a group to test the laws of natural selection, they may eventually come to resemble Eskimos.

Cowboy dress is determined by three factors: weather, work, and vanity. An accountant or businessman who works at a job indoors may alter his

There are two styles of chaps shown here. Author (foreground) is dressed in a pair of full-length shotguns, while Tom Ellzey (right) wears knee-length chinks, or summer leggings.

Hay chaps are not beautiful, but they save the legs a lot of wear and tear when you're handling baled hay.

wardrobe from season to season according to fashion, and what he wears in the summer will not differ drastically from what he wears in the winter. With the cowboy, that's not the case. He works out in the weather and cannot escape the effects of heat and cold; hence what the weather is doing outside will largely determine what he puts on in the morning.

Take his headgear as an example. The cowboy hat is often regarded as a form of plumage, but it also has its functional side. The old-time cowboy may have owned one hat, probably a felt Stetson, which he wore year-round, but most cowboys today have many types of headdress and choose the one that suits the weather best. The traditional felt cowboy hat with the wide, upward-swooping brim is fine for spring and fall work, when the days are neither hot nor cold, and when the cowboy is most likely to need a lid that will shed rainwater. But for all its sartorial splendor, the felt hat is beastly hot in the summertime, and in the winter it is terribly disfunctional in that it offers no protection for the ears.

Along about May or June when the days warm up to ninety or a hundred degrees, most cowboys shed their felt hats and go to one made of straw. The straw hat has many advantages over the felt variety. It is light on the head, its wide brim shades the face and neck from the sun, and its porous crown allows air to pass through, which prevents a large build-up of sweat around the brow. The straw hat is a good piece of equipment, but it has two major disadvantages: it tends to melt in the rain and, because of its light weight, is hard to wear in a high wind.

I have known a few stubborn cowboys who insisted on wearing their felt hats in the dead of winter, and we have all observed that the Marlboro cowboys wear theirs in the snows of the Montana mountains. But many modern cowboys have learned that frostbitten ears are a high price to pay for vanity,

and have adopted the prosaic but warm cap for winter work. (And I would bet that when the picture-taking is over, the Marlboro cowboys hang their cowboy hats on a peg and put on something warmer.) Winter caps have a bill and ear flaps, and might be made of wool, corduroy, or synthetic material. A big seller in western stores these days is the Scotch cap, which has a high crown and colorful markings, and is more attractive than the caps traditionally worn by hunters and farmers. Still, a cap is only a cap, and no matter how warm and functional it may be, the cowboy who wears one is giving up his identity as a man of the West. Where a felt cowboy hat is an earned prize and a badge of honor, the cap is just another piece of clothing that can be worn by anyone. When a cowboy hangs up his straw or felt hat and pulls on his winter cap, he looks dehorned and diminished.

This brings us to the subject of caps in general, and to the debate over whether or not cowboys should wear them. I'm speaking now of the baseball-type caps which, in the past five years, have moved into the West and Southwest and have become almost a regional form of dress. Everyone is wearing a cap these days: bankers, fishermen, hunters, farmers, oil field workers, women, children, professional ropers, and even ranch cowboys. One reason for the popularity of the caps is that they are free. Companies buy them in large quantities, affix the company name or logo on a point just above the base of the bill, and give them to friends and customers.

Caps have become an advertising medium, and the people who wear them have become walking billboards. Ordinary folks are now advertising

Facing page. Left: Cowboy headgear; from top, straw hat, black felt hat, wool Scotch cap, dress felt hat, free cap, and felt hat with rattlesnake-skin band. Top, right: Work spurs. Bottom, right: Strictly functional belt, right, and handmade laced belt for dress, left, that might cost a hundred dollars.

seed companies, fertilizer companies, oil and trucking companies, tractors, banks, and even lariat ropes (Leo Camarillo Ropes). It is an ingenious advertising gimmick, and it may even sell products.

Cowboys were among the last to yield to the temptation of a free cap, for two reasons. First, they balked at the notion of giving up their traditional headdress for a baseball cap. Rodeo ropers were the first of the cowboy crowd to start wearing caps, and they went for them for a sound reason: a cap stays on the head better than a straw or felt hat and doesn't blow off in a windy arena. Since ropers are held in high esteem, their acceptance of the cap made it easier for ranch cowboys to break with tradition, and the cap has become almost fashionable. Once ranch cowboys began wearing caps, they made the same discovery the ropers made: the cap is cool in summer, the bill keeps the sun out of your eyes, and it doesn't blow off in a high wind. There was one further advantage that cowboys were quick to note. A free cap was sixty dollars cheaper than a sixty-dollar Resistol.

A second reason that cowboys were slow to go to the baseball cap was that nobody was in any hurry to give them one. Cowboys are poor consumers. While a farmer may spend a hundred thousand dollars a year on seed, fertilizer, herbicide, tractors, combines, trucks, fuel, and irrigation equipment, a cowboy buys almost nothing. When a farmer purchases a forty-thousand-dollar tractor, it's smart business to give him a two-dollar cap. When a cowboy spends twenty bucks a year on bridle reins and boot repair, it's smart business to tell him "thanks, and hurry back," and to keep the box of free caps under the counter.

But one way or another, they are getting the free caps, and every year at spring roundup you see more and more cowboys wearing them. In February 1979, the *Livestock Weekly* ran a front-page picture of a branding crew in Texas. All seven men wore caps. The caption pointed this out and also noted that the wearing of caps has become a trend in ranch country. A hard core of traditional hatted cowboys has resisted the change, and continues to comment, "If you're going to play baseball, you should carry a bat instead of a rope."

Not all cowboys wear the same type of shirt, but more often than not the shirt will be of the western cut, with the traditional yoke in front and back. It is likely to have snaps instead of buttons, and it will probably be colorful. And it will probably have long sleeves, even in the hottest part of the summer. Many cowboys do not wear short-sleeved shirts, and there is a good reason for it. If a man is out a-horseback, he needs protection from the chill of early morning and late evening, from sunburn in the heat of the day, and from mosquitoes and deer flies that torment him every time he rides through a creek or a river bottom. A short-sleeved shirt would leave him vulnerable to all three. If you're out a-horseback and a long way from home, a long-sleeved shirt is what you want to wear. During the summer months, this shirt will be as light and thin as possible, and made of cotton or cotton-blend fabrics that "breathe." In the fall, when the mornings turn crisp, the cowboy will shift to a shirt made of flannel or wool.

Over his shirt he is likely to wear a vest. Vests are popular with cowboys because they are light and comfortable. They do not bind at the elbows and shoulders, and they give him free use of his arms. A good vest made of down-filled nylon or lined leather is warm and wind-resistant, and as the temperature rises during the day, it can be worn open or tied behind the saddle.

In colder weather the cowboy will wear a jacket over his vest, often a fleece-lined denim jacket which comes to the waist or just below it. At first glance this jacket appears flimsy, and worn by itself it would not provide much protection against the wind-driven cold of the prairie. But it serves as an outer shell, and worn over a lined or down-filled vest, it is adequate. Denim jackets are popular because they are light and comfortable, and also fairly inexpensive. Some cowboys wear a nylon, down-filled coat, similar to those worn by skiers. These are very warm, but also easily torn on barbed wire fences.

The cowboy's pants may bear the name of Levi's, Lee's, Wranglers, Big Smith, or Sears, but they will always be jeans made of heavy cotton fabric. Occasionally you find a rancher who wears khaki pants, but the cowboys I have known always dressed in jeans. This is one article of clothing that they never talk about. There is no argument and no discussion. Jeans are cut right, they fit right, they feel right. They must have been made for cowboys.

There is another advantage to jeans that I have never heard anyone mention, and which I discovered by accident. I went out on horseback one afternoon wearing a pair of dress pants that I had bought on sale. At seven dollars, they seemed a good substitute for a pair of fourteen-dollar jeans. These pants were made of a synthetic fabric and contained little or no cotton. After several hours of riding, I discovered that it is difficult to stay in the saddle when you're wearing pants made of synthetic fabric. The man-made fibers are so slick that they slide over the surface of the saddle, making it hard for the rider to maintain his balance when his horse turns sharply or moves across rough terrain. Most cowboys are not aware of it, but the cotton in their jeans makes them better horsemen.

The cowboy wears his jeans winter and summer. He wears his newest jeans, the ones that are stiffest and thickest, in the winter when he needs warmth, and he goes to his thin ones in the summer, when a hole here and there merely makes for better air conditioning. If he has a loving wife, he may get two years' wear out of a pair of jeans. A woman's love can often be seen in the patches she has sewn into her husband's pants.

Many cowboys don't even own a pair of shoes, or if they do they never take them out of the closet. Boots are well suited for the cowboy's life and work. If he wore low-topped shoes on the job, his socks would soon bristle with stickers and weed seeds, his shoes would be full of sand, and he would be loath to take a step lest he be struck on the ankle by a rattlesnake lurking in the weeds. High-topped boots protect him from these hazards.

There are many types and styles of boots, and his closet will probably be stacked with four or five pairs, each with its own function or season of wear. My summer boot is a Wellington-type boot made of elk-tanned cowhide and treated with oil instead of polish. This boot has a neoprene sole and a low heel, and it is suited for summer jobs that require good traction, such as climbing windmill towers, standing on hay stacks, or walking fence. It is extremely durable, and I have never really worn a pair out. I stop wearing them when I want a new pair of boots, or when the old pair begins to smell up the house.

Then there is the riding boot, one which is specifically designed for use a-horseback. Every cowboy has his own taste in boots, and some don't mind using the same boot for foot-work and horseback-work. I prefer a special pair for riding, and I never wear them except when I'm a-horseback. My riding boots have a tall, underslung heel that, in theory at least, keeps the foot from going through the stirrup. The soles are made of leather, and the tops come up to mid-calf and keep the saddle from rubbing my legs.

A riding boot should be comfortable and heavy enough to hold a spur, but its primary purpose is to give the cowboy some insurance against getting hung up and dragged. My riding boot has a slick leather sole which will slide easily out of a stirrup in an emergency. But in the event the boot does go into the stirrup, I want a big heel that will keep my foot from going all the way through. If my horse starts bucking or falls to the ground, I want my feet to come free of the stirrups, and a boot that will slip out of a stirrup is a good investment.

I have a boot for summer wear, and I also have a boot which I wear only in cold winter weather. It is an Acme rough-out boot with a walking heel that is suited for the winter jobs, which usually revolve around feeding cattle. The only distinctive feature of this boot is that it is two sizes larger than my summer boot. I wear a thin sock in the summer, but in the winter I need the warmth of a thin sock and a heavy wool sock. The extra length in the winter boot gives my foot plenty of room and prevents loss of circulation.

But this is a poor man's solution to the problem of cold feet, and it is adequate only if the winter is dry. One morning in the snow, and these boots are worthless. When snow enters the picture, the cowboy must take steps to keep his feet dry. One option lies in buying a pair of overshoes that he can wear over his boots. Another lies in shopping around for a good pair of insulated rubber boots. Every winter I study the catalog of the L. L. Bean Company, a manufacturer of sport and outdoor equipment in Maine. Since Bean is based in snowy New England, and since the company is in the business of designing and making equipment that will keep outdoorsmen warm and dry, I consider the Bean catalog an excellent source of information on the subject. Bean makes a winter boot which was designed for snowmobilers and ice fishermen. It has a rubber body and sole, a leather upper, and comes with a thick felt liner that can be removed at night and dried. It is an aesthetic horror, but appears to provide all the protection a man would need in the winter.

The last category of boots is the cowboy's pair of dress boots. These are reserved for special occasions when he wants to appear neat and somewhat civilized, occasions which come along so seldom that a pair of dress boots may last ten years or more. They are kept polished and shiny, and the same cowboy who would think nothing of wearing his work boots through the muck of a wet cow lot picks his path as carefully as a cat when he has his good boots on his feet.

Dress boots are expensive, and they are getting more so every year. Plain vanilla runs about a hundred dollars today, in 1980. Boots made of more exotic leathers (kangaroo, camel, shark, antelope) range up to one hundred and fifty dollars, and the real exotics (boa constrictor, lizard, and ostrich) might cost two or three hundred dollars. Boots manufactured by the Luchese Boot Company of San Antonio are almost entirely handmade and are considered the Rolls Royce of the boot world. They are priced around two to three hundred dollars, and I have never seen a pair of them on a ranch cowboy.

Cowboys have always been very particular about what they wore on their feet, but the price of being well shod is getting more painful all the time. The cost of leather and leather products is rising with inflation, and cowboy wages aren't. In the years to come, one of the most important figures in a ranching community will undoubtedly be the cobbler who can half-sole, re-heel, and patch that old pair of boots and give it another six months of life.

Another leather item in the cowboy's wardrobe is his belt. For most men, a belt is something which holds up his pants. Typically, cowboys have expanded on its function and made it into another expression of male and professional vanity. A cowboy's belt is usually wide, made of good leather, and often adorned with tooling, the cowboy's name, or some fancy stitching. My most treasured belt was handmade by Tom Ellzey of the LZ Ranch

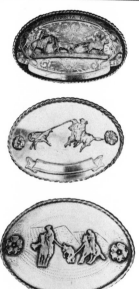

Some of the trophy buckles Jake Parker has won in the roping arena.

A good look at this cowboy's trophy belt buckle.

in Texas, who wove and braided ten yards of leather lacing into swirls and patterns, and raised this humble pants-holder-upper into a work of high craftsmanship.

Every belt must have a buckle, and once again the cowboy transforms function into peacockery. His everyday buckle might be made of heavy brass, while his dress buckle might contain gold, sterling silver, and even semi-precious and precious stones. I have seen six-hundred-dollar buckles advertised in western wear catalogs. But the very best and most esteemed buckles are those that were purchased with flesh, blood, tears, and sweat—trophy buckles won in rodeo competition. A cowboy who has to buy his buckles isn't as proud of it, knowing that no matter how much he pays or how fine the workmanship, his buckle is just a consumer item and will lack the aura and instant respect a prize buckle commands. Trophy buckles are the equivalent of war medals, and cowboys who wear them are soldiers who have proved themselves under fire. A trophy buckle won in bronc or bull riding tells the world that this fellow is a good rider; it may also help explain his bridgework or the odd shape of his nose or why he walks like a crab. A buckle won in roping competition marks a man as an expert in the skill cowboys most admire and covet. Cowboys check out those trophy buckles.

Gloves are part of a cowboy's everyday dress, and you rarely see one without a pair of gloves on his hands, in his hip pocket, or tucked under his belt. Most cowboys have a standard pair of gloves which they carry with them. The leather is soft and pliable, and it may be split cowhide, mule hide, horse hide, pigskin, or elk hide. A pair of these gloves will range in price from seven dollars for a pair that doesn't fit well to fifteen dollars for a pair of good heavy elk hides. Cheap gloves are a constant irritant. The thumb is in the wrong place, the finger holes are always too big, and the stitching begins to unravel in the second or third week of wear. You never wear out cheap gloves; they merely disintegrate on your hands. To get gloves that have good leather and good stitching, you have to pay ten to fifteen dollars, and even these will not last six months under normal conditions. Any cowboy who gets six months' wear out of a pair of gloves shouldn't be trusted.

When the cowboy is handling barbed wire, he needs a heavier glove to protect his hands from sharp and rusted barbs. A good fencing glove has a palm made of heavy split cowhide and a cuff, made of a stiff canvaslike material, that comes up three or four inches above the wrist. Leather welding gloves are good for fence work.

Windmill work presents a different set of problems, and the cowboy may choose a different type of glove. You don't want to wear expensive leather gloves around a windmill. In pulling the rods out of the hole, your gloves become soaked with water and with the muck that collects on the jet rods. Moisture leaves the leather stiff and brittle and rots out the stitching. It's not a bad idea to use cheap cotton gloves for windmill work. When they get soaked up with mud and grease, you just throw them away. And you can buy five pairs of cotton gloves for the price of one good pair made of leather.

If the cowboy does much roping, he may have a special pair of gloves that he uses for nothing else. This glove will be thin and tight-fitting so that he does not lose the feel of the rope. Roping is a science of inches and seconds, and a heavy, awkward glove can mean the difference between a catch and a miss. Gloves made of calfskin, deerskin, and goatskin are too fragile for most forms of ranch work, but they serve the roper's purpose quite well.

There is no labor on a ranch that tears up gloves faster than work in a hay field, especially if you pick up the bales by the wires instead of using hay hooks. If you load and unload five hundred bales a day, you have applied from three to five tons of weight and friction to the leather on the inside of the fingers. You also sweat a great deal, and much of that sweat ends up in your gloves. This combination of water, salt, weight, and friction destroys gloves in a matter of days. If you use cheap cotton gloves, you merely wear out your hands. If you use good leather gloves, you spare yourself the pain of blisters and splinters only to feel the pain of buying a new pair of gloves.

Chaps, or leggings, are another specialized form of cowboy dress. Chaps, like almost everything else in the cowboy's closet and saddle room, originated in Mexico, where they were called *chaparejos*. Full-length riding chaps come in two styles: shotguns, which fit closely around the legs and zip up in the back, and batwings, which buckle in the back and fit loosely on the legs. There was a time, perhaps forty or fifty years ago, when batwings were the preferred style, and most pictures of old-time cowboys show them wearing batwings. But for some reason, they seem to have gone out of style, and most of the cowboys in our part of the country wear shotguns. Chaps are usually made of soft leather, either split cowhide with a suede look to it or leather with a smooth finish. You can order chaps in any color you choose, but the colors usually reflect the colors found in the prairie country in winter: brown, tan, black, and orange. Rodeo riders often wear a type of modified batwing chaps in colors that run to bright reds, greens, and blues, but these colors are rarely seen on a roundup crew. I suppose it is a matter of taste, and the taste of ranch cowboys follows the quiet colors of the country itself.

You can buy ready-made chaps in most western wear stores, or order them out of a catalog, but the ones I have seen in the stores were of inferior quality and made of stiff, heavy leather. The best way to buy chaps is to find a boot or saddle shop where they are made from scratch. You can go in and choose the style, color, and leather you want. The maker will take measurements of your thigh, waist, and stride, and make the chaps to fit. Custom-made chaps may cost more than the store-bought variety, but they are well worth the difference in price. My favorite pair of shotguns was made by Reid Errington, a saddlemaker in Canadian, Texas. I ordered them in 1978 and paid eighty dollars for them. At the time, I was working on a ranch in the Oklahoma Panhandle and making six hundred a month, so an eighty-dollar pair of chaps was a large investment for me. But I have never regretted my decision to buy the best.

Cowboys wear chaps for a variety of reasons. Chaps provide a layer of leather armor that protects his legs from stobs, thorns, and limbs when he is riding in brush. If his horse passes too close to a barbed wire fence (and some horses will do this on purpose to intimidate the rider), a pair of chaps can save him the price of a new pair of jeans and maybe part of a leg. During fall and spring roundup seasons, when the mornings are crisp and the weather tends to be unpredictable, chaps will keep his legs warm and dry even if a wet norther comes rolling in. In a branding pen, chaps offer a certain amount of protection from kicking calves and from misguided vaccinating needles, dehorning tubes, and castrating knives.

There is another reason why cowboys wear chaps: they are part of his traditional dress, and they are fun to wear. A pair of chaps made of good leather and kept soft with regular applications of neat's-foot oil is an object of beauty. I have pulled on my chaps hundreds of times, yet it has never become a dull routine. There is a certain thrill to it that cannot be found anywhere else. Maybe a business executive feels the same way when he buttons up the vest of his Brooks Brothers suit, gazes at himself in the mirror, and knows that he is dressed for something better than a dog fight. To me, wearing chaps is one of the little honors of the profession. If you haven't earned the honor, you appear absurd; but if you have, you become a knight in armor. Maybe that's what makes chaps so special: you have to earn the right to wear them. In this day and time, money will buy almost anything, including a Brooks Brothers suit. But while you might buy your way into a pair of chaps, you can't buy the dignity and the pride that go with them. That belongs only to the cowboys who have wrecked a few horses and roped a few cows, who have felt some pain and taken some risks and squeezed up some courage from deep down inside. You might say that what fills a pair of chaps is not two skinny legs, but the quality of the man who wears them.

When hot weather comes, most cowboys leave their chaps hanging on a peg in the saddle room. They make the legs sweat, and they hold in heat that needs to be expired. There is a style of chaps, called summer leggings, or "chinks," which is made for use in hot weather. They are cut off just below the knee and are open at the back. We don't see them much in the high plains country. I have seen cowboys wearing them in the hot, brushy country around Del Rio, Texas, and in his book of color photographs, *Cowboys of the High Sierra,* Peter Perkins has a number of shots that show California cowboys wearing summer leggings. Whether the boys in California wear them as protection against brush or strictly for looks, I don't know.

There is one last style of chaps which we should mention, and that is the hay chaps. Anyone who handles large amounts of hay soon learns that bales of hay, and especially alfalfa, chew up blue jeans and hide at a brisk pace. This problem can be corrected with a pair of hay chaps that are usually made of stiff and unlovely cowhide, and which can be bought for just about what a new pair of jeans would cost. They fit loosely about the legs and are not unendurably hot in a hay field. They're not beautiful, and the cowboy feels no particular joy or pride in wearing them, but they serve a purpose. After you have worn hay chaps for a while, the thought of handling hay without them is unbearable.

The last piece of specialized cowboy apparel we will consider is the spur which comes in many sizes and shapes. Calf ropers who are competing against the clock and who must run down the rope to throw a calf prefer a very small and light spur. Bull riders in rodeo use a spur that is specially designed for their event. It has a fixed rowel that is used to dig into and grip the loose hide of a bucking bull. Ranch cowboys, who are not competing in a timed event or riding bucking stock, have a wider choice of styles. They may choose a heavy spur with a big, vulgar, jingling rowel, or they may select a style that is smaller, lighter, and less ostentatious. The big spurs are fun to wear, and they may even have some advantages if a cowboy is mounted on a stubborn horse. But in a branding pen, where he is walking to the branding fire and wrestling calves, the big spurs can be awkward and heavy on his feet.

Spurs perform three functions. On a bucking horse, they can be locked into the cinch to give the cowboy better balance and a more secure seat in the saddle. This function was more important back in the old days when cowboys rode green-broke and rough string horses and could expect some action anytime they climbed aboard. But today's horses are better behaved, and the gripping function of spurs has declined in importance.

Spurs can also be used to punish a horse, and the classic example of this can be seen in bareback bronc riding. In this event, the cowboy drives his spurs into the horse's shoulders on every jump, in effect punishing him for bucking. A horse that can't take a spurring will figure this out and quit. Of course, rodeo horses are a special case. They are chosen precisely because they are outlaws, and if a bronc ever reaches the point where he can't take a spurring, he will lose his job. In ranch work, spurs are used only occasionally as instruments of punishment, and only when there is a good reason for it. In my years of ranch work, I have never seen an instance where a horse was injured by a pair of spurs. The worst effects I have observed on a spurred horse were "tracks" on the shoulders, marks left on the hair, which did not penetrate the hide or draw blood. Now and then you hear about cowboys who sharpened their spur rowels with a file and used them to "tune up" a stubborn horse. You hear about those things, but you never see them.

The ranch cowboy will occasionally use his spurs to grip and to punish, but most of the time he uses them only to get the attention of his mount. Horses, like their masters, tend to drift into sloth, torpor, and mediocrity if left to their own devices. We humans are goaded into action by our spouses, bosses, and those anonymous villains who keep sending us bills in the mail. Horses are goaded by spurs. Some horses don't need spurs and should not be ridden with them. They have the spirit and the motivation to do their work, and spurring will only make them nervous and hyperactive. But most horses do need the goad of spurs. A nudge of spurs tells them that it's time to move out and go to work. Properly used, the spur is a medium of communication between horse and rider.

The modern cowboy, like his old-time counterpart, chooses his clothes to suit the job and the weather, yet he continues to show an uncanny knack for transforming what he wears into plumage. Watching cowboys strut at a spring roundup is one of the rewards of being in this business.

3

The Cowboy's Wife

When a woman marries a cowboy, she is choosing something other than a life of ease and luxury.

It has been observed that the West was hell on horses and women. As far as the cowboy was concerned, it was also hell on the institution of marriage.

Not only were women in short supply in the Old West, but the cowboy who lived in an isolated cow camp and ventured into town once a month was in no position to go courting. And even if he had been able to go courting and had managed to find the girl of his dreams, he would have taken a wife and lost a job. Most of the old ranches were not set up to accommodate wives and families among the hired hands, and when the cowboy married, it was understood that he would have to move on. This practice began in the earliest days of the cattle industry when life on a frontier ranch was too spartan for women and children, and later, say by 1890, it evolved into ranch policy and endured because of its economic benefits to the rancher.

And there were several economic benefits. Single men were "good keepers"; their needs were simple and they required no special luxuries. In the case of the headquarters cowboys, four or five of them could room together in the same bunkhouse, and they could be fed the same fare at the same table. In the case of camp cowboys, one or two men lived in a line-camp shack and prepared their own simple meals. In neither case did the ranch have much of an investment in room and board. In those days, it probably cost more to keep and feed a good saddle horse than to maintain a good cowboy. The introduction of women into this environment would have complicated things. A woman would have wanted her own house and yard. She would have wanted to add on a spare bedroom or a screened-in porch, which would have required the rancher to come up with lumber, paint, and nails. Bachelor cowboys were preferred because they made fewer demands than married men, and they cost less money.

But there were other factors that tended to discourage the cowboy from taking a wife. His way of life was just not suited to the schedules of children and the needs of a wife. The isolation, the long hours, the low wages, and the hazards of the job tended to attract a certain type of man, and in most cases he was not the type who wanted to marry and settle down. Sure, he made up mournful songs about the girl he left behind, but instead of going back to get her and marry her and build her a little house, he chose to sing about her in a place where there was no danger that he would have to give substance to his poetry. His life as a cowboy was simple and carefree, and he was there because that's what he wanted.

As far as I can determine, the bachelor cowboy began to disappear from small and medium-sized ranches around 1950, and today the old bunkhouse has either rotted into the ground or has become a storage shed that catches the overflow from the rancher's house. The bachelor cowboys were replaced by married men, and the bunkhouse gave way to the tenant house, a small, simple dwelling which could accommodate a woman and children.

Why did this change occur around 1950? By that time motorized pickups had replaced wagons, tractors had replaced teams of horses, and machinery had begun doing jobs which, up until then, had been done by manual labor. Large crews of men were no longer necessary. One man with a pickup and stock trailer could feed and look after five or six hundred cows, an operation that once had required the efforts of three or four men. With this increase in productivity made possible by machinery, the rancher was more inclined to spend money on a permanent house for the hired hand, and to offer a few conveniences that would attract the kind of man who was married, stable, and settled.

Of course there was another side to this. The men who had gone off to the war had seen Par-ee and a few other cities, and perhaps the lure of the cow camp had begun to fade. The postwar economy was booming, high-paying jobs could be had, and the American dream of a little house in the suburbs was within easy reach of a man with a good job and a G.I. loan. Country boys packed their bags and headed for the cities, and the pool of cowboy labor began to dry up. Prosperity brought choices. If a man didn't want to be a hermit and a bachelor, if he didn't want to live in a barracks with other men, if he didn't want to put up with the unpleasant side of cowboy life, he didn't have to. He could become a welder or a salesman or a small businessman, marry and start a family, and build up an equity in his own property. Ranchers had to respond to this labor market, and were forced to sweeten their deals and to offer their cowboys more than a bunkhouse bed and a side of beef.

These changes revolutionized the ranching business, and we might even say that the era of the Old West ended, not with the introduction of barbed wire and windmills, but with the passing of the bachelor cowboy and the bunkhouse. Depending on your perspective, it was a quantum leap either forward or backward. Writers, artists, and poets will mourn the change. Cowboys, who rather enjoy the luxury of having children, will regard the change as progressive. But good or bad, the bachelor cowboy has virtually disappeared from the American West, and barring some economic catastrophe, he will probably never return. I began working on ranches in 1959 and have cowboyed off and on for twenty years. During that time I have worked with only two bachelor cowboys. I have met several others, but by the time I strapped on my spurs, most of them had already gone into retirement.

Today's cowboy is a married man. In many respects the quality of his life has vastly improved over what it would have been forty years ago. But he also has problems that the old-time cowboy never had to face. He has a wife now, and he is no longer in a position to think only of himself and his own simple needs.

When a woman marries a cowboy, she is choosing something other than a life of ease and luxury. The first adjustment she must make on a ranch hits her the very first day she moves into the tenant house: the house is not hers. It belongs to the owners of the ranch. It may be a small but nice frame house or a new mobile home. It also might be a stinking hovel with grease on the walls and mice in the drawers, cockroaches, spiders, ants, snakes, holes in the walls, cracked windows, rusted and bulging screens, and dripping water pipes. This is where she will live and spend her days and nights, where she will prepare her meals and raise her children and try to make a home. If the boss is generous, he may offer some kind of housing allowance. If he's not generous, he will offer nothing, thus forcing her to use her own labor and meager funds to make the place livable, or to complain and beg for every little improvement she needs. As she goes through her everyday chores in the kitchen, washroom, and bedrooms, she is reminded over and over that the house isn't hers, it will never be hers, and anything she does to make it express her tastes and needs is subject to higher approval and criticism.

For the woman, country living can be difficult and inconvenient. In 1978–79, we lived on a ranch in the Oklahoma Panhandle, thirty miles from the nearest town. Scottie was four years old and Ashley was a pup of six months. Together, they generated a lot of dirty clothes. In the fall of the year, when I was working from daylight to dark on a roundup crew, the washing machine broke down. Kris had to call a serviceman to come out and fix it so that she could stay ahead of the mountain of dirty diapers. The serviceman was busy with jobs in town and wasn't much interested in making a call out in the bojacks, but several days later he drove out. After five minutes' work with a screwdriver, he discovered that the problem was a broken belt. He replaced the four-dollar belt and presented Kris with a bill for forty bucks—two days' wages for me.

About this same time the sewer line stopped up, which shut down the bathtub, the toilet, the washer, and the kitchen sink. Again, the diapers began piling up, and everyone was running out into the trees to answer the calls of nature. We just couldn't afford another service call, so one foul, drizzly day a friend and I had to stop what we were doing and try to fix it. By the middle of the afternoon, after hacking several holes in the frozen ground and checking the sewer line in several spots, we located the problem: tree roots near the south side of the house. We built our own crude Roto-rooter out of a half-inch electric drill and a long piece of cable and opened the line.

Not long after this we had a cold, wet spell. The roads became slick with mud, then deeply rutted by four-wheel-drive vehicles. When Kris made trips to town with sick children or to get groceries, she had to drive one of our two little cars, a Pinto and a Vega. Together, they did not quite add up to one good, reliable car. Both were built low to the ground and would high-center on a mole hill, and neither was very good in mud. Somehow Kris always managed to plow her way to the blacktop, and then to make it back home, but the rough roads beat our little cars to pieces. By Christmas, the Pinto had a bent frame and no muffler, and the Vega was suffering from some cancerous malady that eventually cost us a new motor.

After New Year's Day, snow covered the ground for a month and the temperature at night fell to ten below zero. The drain on the washing machine froze up and the cursed thing flooded the utility room. Kris wept while I began the cleanup operation. During this cold spell neither of our cars would start. The Pinto developed a solenoid problem, while the battery on the Vega went dead. Kris was trying to take Scot into a preschool in Beaver twice a week so that he would have a chance to meet and play with children his own age, since he had lived on ranches all his life and had spent most of his time around adults. The combination of cold, snow, mud, ruts, and poor automobiles made her trips to town all but impossible. Yet somehow she managed.

In February the snow began to melt and we found ourselves living in a muddy swamp. Kris did her best to keep the mud outside where it belonged, but inevitably some of it found its way into the house. By this time the motor in the Vega had thrashed, Scottie got an ear infection, I had holes in my gloves and overshoes, and we were getting regular overdraft notices from the bank. One Friday afternoon we had a blowing snow from the north. By Saturday afternoon it appeared the roads were passable, and since we all had cabin fever, we loaded up into the Pinto and went to visit our friends Sandy and Geneva Hagar, who lived on a ranch twelve miles away. The road was clear except for one spot where it had drifted two feet deep. We stuck the car. I carried Scottie and Kris carried Ashley to the nearest house. The temperature was eight degrees. We never made it to the Hagars'.

Those same country roads that make it hard for the cowboy's wife to get into town also discourage her friends in town from driving out to visit. Women who live in town and who are accustomed to reaching any destination in five minutes may look upon a drive out into the country as a safari. They may worry about car trouble or getting lost. The cowboy's wife has learned to cope with these problems because they have been forced upon her. Town women have the choice of going or not going, and they may find that it is easier and safer to stay home or to keep up with friends down the street. This tends to isolate the cowboy's wife and to limit her social contacts to other women who live in the country.

Another factor which may contribute to her isolation is the community's opinion of her husband's profession. In many communities a cowboy is regarded as a mere hired hand, and his wife may encounter snubs that remind her that she belongs to the hired hand class and that she should not hope to associate with her "betters."

We have already seen that the cowboy is defined by his work, yet his wife does not really fit into the everyday operation of the ranch. I have known many wives of *ranchers* who pitched in and helped with the work. On short notice, they might be called upon to ride horseback, feed cattle, build fence, or work in the hay field. But ranch wives have a stake in the business, and their place on the ranch is clearly defined. The position of the cowboy's wife is ambiguous. She lives on the ranch, but it is not hers. If she helps her husband with his work, she knows that she probably won't be paid for it, and that she is simply contributing her time and labor to the greater glory of the outfit. If she feels that her time is worth something—and why not? Other people are charging her for *their* time—she may choose to do something for herself and stay home.

But there is another reason why the wife of the cowboy does not often participate in the ranch work: cowboying is, and always has been, a man's world. When the woman enters this world, she senses that she is intruding and creating an awkward situation. Larry McMurtry, a keen observer of ranch life, has said that the cowboy is committed "to a heroic concept of life that simply takes little account of women. . . . Most of them marry, and love their wives sincerely, but since their sociology idealizes women and their mythology excludes her, the impasse which results is often little short of tragic" (*In a Narrow Grave: Essays on Texas,* pp. 148, 150).

McMurtry has put his finger on a sensitive nerve. Fifty years ago it didn't make much difference how the cowboy viewed women because there weren't many women around. Today, most cowboys are married. They take their women to isolated ranches, put them in houses that don't belong to them, and then expect them to adjust to a way of life that leaves them in emotional limbo. Young women today are not as inclined to accept this as their mothers and grandmothers were, and this is producing tension in the tenant house. I have seen many a young cowboy leave the profession to save his marriage, and others who did not leave soon enough. One of the quickest ways to lose a cowboy is to make his wife unhappy, for to one degree or another she must give her consent to his way of life. I have an idea that in years to come, both ranchers and cowboys will be forced to give more thought to this matter than they have in the past.

4

Horse Sense and Cow Sense

*Each breed is different, each herd is differ-
ent, each day is different.*

The cowboy has always been a man-of-the-horse, and in the year 1980,
horsemanship remains a critical skill. Contrary to some popular notions, he
doesn't spend all his waking hours a-horseback. Fifty years ago, he might
have. Today he doesn't. But when he does climb into the saddle, he had
better know how to handle a horse under all conditions, because the horse
remains the most important tool on a cattle ranch.

Horsemanship consists of many elements and subskills which are not visi-
ble to the outside observer. The cowboy must possess some understanding
of how horses think and why they behave as they do. As the old saying goes,
he ought to be smarter than his horse. That statement, often made in jest,
contains a kernel of truth, because many times poor horsemanship derives
from a misunderstanding of the animal. Horses are highly predictable. You
can predict that when a horse is full of green grass and hasn't been ridden in
a while, he will try to buck. You can predict that when horses are eating together, they will kick and bite each other, and that if you slip up behind one,
he might kick you through the side of the saddle room. You can predict that
a green colt will shy at strange objects; that a mare in heat will be temperamental and hard to handle; that a stud horse will try either to fight or to breed
any horse around him; that if you leave a gate unlatched, even for a few

minutes, horses will find it and go where they are not supposed to go; that most horses will resist being caught and bridled; and that if you don't control the horse, he will control you.

All horses have habits and patterns of behavior. They all have flaws and limitations. The good horseman is one who understands the general psychology of horses and also the specific quirks of the ones in his string. He must have some compassion for the beast and for his weaknesses, so that he doesn't ask him to perform impossible feats. But he must also know what the horse *can* do, and then coax or force him to do it.

Next, he must be familiar with equestrian hardware and equipment—bits, bridles, tie-downs, pads, saddles, roping equipment, and cinches. If you use a bit that is too severe on a colt, you can deaden the bars in his mouth and make him iron-jawed (hard to stop). But if he's iron-jawed already, you may have to use a severe bit. If he has a tendency to throw his head, or if he carries his head too high, you may need to use a tie-down. If he develops sores under the saddle, you might have to wash the salt out of your saddle pad or buy a new one. If he galls along his belly, you may need to put some padding on the cinch. If the horse gets sore-footed, he may need shoes. If he has a tendency to stumble, he may need his feet trimmed.

Over the centuries, man has developed a whole technology that is devoted to the care and handling of horses. A book could be written about the horse's mouth, with a section devoted to the various types of bits (curbs, snaffles, breaking bits, cutting horse bits, corrective bits), and other sections covering halters, hackamores, bosals, and other hardware. It would take another book to deal with the science of caring for the horse's feet: anatomy, injuries, shoeing, corrective shoeing, shoeing for special jobs, farrier's tools, and trimming. Most cowboys are not experts in either field but have a working familiarity with both, and have acquired enough knowledge and expertise to solve the ordinary problems they encounter.

The third ingredient in good horsemanship is athletic ability, which includes balance, strength, reaction time, and endurance. In limited quantities, horseback riding can be considered an amusement and a sport, but when it is done professionally, when the rider spends from eight to twelve hours a day in the saddle, it becomes hard, demanding work. The cowboy must possess the hand, arm, and shoulder strength to manhandle a horse that tries to buck or take the bit, enough endurance and muscle tone to take the pounding of a rough horse, the balance to keep himself in the saddle over all terrain and at all speeds, and the quick reactions to respond to sudden danger.

And finally, a good horseman must have courage that is tempered with common sense. He should have the courage to do his work in spite of the hazards, but also enough sense and judgment to avoid accidents and keep himself healthy for another day's work.

Another important cowboy skill involves his knowledge and understanding of the cow brute, which often goes under the name of "cow sense" or "cow psychology." This is knowledge that cannot be gotten from a book, but only from years of experience and careful observation. The best cowboys have cow sense, while others never seem to pick it up. I have known cowboys who have worked for years on ranches and still couldn't predict what a cow brute was going to do. Of one of these characters, a friend of mine once observed in disgust, "He just don't think like livestock." To some cowboys, it seems to come easily and naturally, while others never seem to learn the signs.

There is no single rule or sign that will apply to all classes of cattle. First of

Success in a job often means matching the work to the right horse. The author is about to rope a stray heifer, and for the task he has chosen a stocky quarter horse mare that is educated to the rope.

all, you have many breeds of beef cattle: Herefords, Angus, Brangus, Brahman, Charolais, Simmental, Santa Gertrudis, shorthorn, longhorn, and others. Each breed of cattle tends to show a certain temperament and behave in a certain way, and the cowboy will not handle one breed in exactly the same way he would handle another.

When I approach Hereford cattle, I assume that they will have a fairly gentle disposition and will be easy to handle. That is not true in every case, but it is true enough to work as a general principle. When I work around Angus cattle, especially in a set of pens, I am aware that black cattle are more prone to kick than any other breed. Again, this is not true 100 percent of the time, but if you ask a cowboy or a truck driver about black cattle, the first thing he will tell you is that they are kickers. When I approach any cow brute with a thin nose, long ears, and a hump in its neck, characteristics which show Brahman breeding, I move with caution, because it is my experience that Brahman-type animals are often quick and unpredictable. It isn't always true, but it's true enough.

I have said that Hereford cattle generally have a good disposition and are easy to handle. That's usually the case, but not always. One herd of Herefords may be gentle, while another may be every bit as waspy as anything that ever walked on four legs and said moo. The cowboy not only has to know the general temperament of the breed, but also the temperament and habits of each particular herd. Through experience or through the grapevine, he learns the reputation of a ranch's cow herd, and even of the cattle in separate pastures. Cattle in a small upland pasture might be easy to handle, while the cattle across the fence in a big river pasture—on the same ranch and out of the same bloodlines—might be as wild as rabbits.

The weather conditions also go into the cowboy's equation. In cool weather or in the morning, cattle are more prone to run than they are in hot weather or in the afternoon, while in hot weather they are more likely to sull and fight. Snow can affect their behavior. It is difficult to drive cattle into a wind-driven snowstorm, and if snow has been on the ground for several days, the cattle may be sore-footed, in which case they might not want to move. I have also heard cowboys say that cattle are affected by barometric pressure, and that they can be hard to handle when a low-pressure system has moved into the area.

Each breed is different, each herd is different, each day is different. And each class and type of animal is different. Cows, meaning adult breeding females, are usually cooperative. They have some age on them, which means that they have been gathered and rounded up before. They have seen men a-horseback, they know the ranch routine, and they have outgrown the silliness of youth. Unless they have been soured or spoiled by cowboys who didn't know their business, cows are generally easy to handle.

Bulls are a different matter. They are larger than cows, and as a group they tend to have a bad attitude. If a bull is old and heavy, his feet may be in poor condition and he will move very slowly. To get him in motion, the cowboy might have to take down his rope and pop him on the rump. A younger, healthier bull must be treated with respect. Some bulls simply don't want to be gathered, and when they have gone as far as they want to go, they will turn and fight. A fighting bull is a nuisance and a health hazard. If you quit him and leave him in the pasture, he will be twice as hard to handle the next time you gather the herd. For that reason some ranchers have a standing policy of never allowing a bull to escape a roundup. If he won't go to the corral under his own power, they rope him and drag him into a stock trailer and deliver him to the pens. I heard about a rancher in the Oklahoma Panhandle who employed a novel gambit in dealing with fighting bulls: he shot them in the pasture and sold them, range delivery, to a butcher in town.

Yearling steers and heifers are fairly unpredictable. They are young and frisky, and while they may handle easily one day, they may be pure hell to gather the next. Freshly weaned cattle or cattle that have been shipped in from the South can be easily spooked by sudden movements or loud noises—a passing car or airplane, a cowboy who sneezes, a horse that stumbles. Once frightened, they behave like minnows, each animal following the one in front of him. It often happens that the animal in the lead is the one who is least qualified to provide leadership. He might be blind in one or both eyes or simply crazy. For that reason, yearlings are notorious for flattening fences, widening gates, running through and over cowboys, and tearing up corrals.

Baby calves can also be difficult to manage, and their psychology is entirely different from that of any other class of cattle. As a general rule, a cow and calf will always travel together. If they become separated, the cow will begin bawling for her calf and the calf will bawl for its mother. Until they are reunited, they are both unstable and hard to handle. Newborn calves don't have a lick of sense. Frightened by the appearance of a man on horseback, a fresh calf might take off running in any direction, and he might run for a mile or more, going through every fence that he comes to. Baby calves in this frenzied state are impossible to control. You can't turn them or stop them, and about all you can do is rope them and take them back to their mothers.

An experienced cowboy is always alert and looking for trouble when he is gathering cattle. He concentrates on his business and doesn't allow his mind to wander, and he can see a wreck coming before it ever happens. He can look at a herd of cattle and tell you what is on their mind. In the background, he has his knowledge of breed, class of cattle, and weather conditions, and to this he keeps adding readings from the animals in front of him. Cattle usually show their thoughts and feelings in outward signs. The cowboy studies their eyes, their ears, their tails, and the angle at which they hold their heads. A waspy cow will reveal herself with a high head, wide eyes, and cocked ears, and an alert cowboy can scan a herd of cattle and pick her out in an instant.

The cowboy applies his knowledge of cattle in other ways. An important part of his job lies in his ability to judge the health and condition of the cattle he looks after, and in spotting trouble before it develops. Any time he drives or rides through the herd he is looking for signs. A full udder on a cow might mean that she has lost her calf. A cow that is thin or hollow-eyed might be sick or so old that she can't keep herself in good condition. A cow that stays off to herself should always be checked. A calf with droopy ears may have ear ticks, a head cold, or pneumonia. A calf that shakes his head may have maggots working in the wounds where he was dehorned. A calf with a bulge on the left side of its abdomen might be bloated. A bull that doesn't breed cows or that spends too much time under a shade tree isn't earning his keep and should be sold. A cow with a watery eye may have cancer-eye, while a calf with the same symptom is likely to have pinkeye.

The experienced cowboy is constantly looking for these problems, and he can pick the problem animals out of a herd the instant he sees them. The cowboys who are the best judges of cattle have strong powers of concentration and excellent memories. I have known men who could look at a herd of a hundred cows, all of the same color, size, and shape, and tell you which cow was missing. That is an amazing feat, and I have never mastered it myself.

A cowboy seems to be a man who wears a big hat and a pair of jingling spurs, who rides off to work on a horse and yells at cattle. He is also a highly trained observer who, in the course of a normal day, must read the minds of animals that aren't particularly bright and can't talk.

5

Cowboy Vices and Recreation

Cowboys have always been slaves to tobacco, but the modern cowboy does not use it in the same forms that the old-time punchers did. In his book *The Cowboy*, Philip Rollins declares that smoking was universal among the old-timers, while chewing "was common but far from universal" (pp. 85–86). Of course the old punchers always rolled their own smokes, and in typical cowboy manner of raising nonsense to the level of folk art, they took great pride in rolling their cigarettes. The best of them could do it with only one hand.

But things have changed a great deal out west. Mr. Rollins would be startled to learn that, on a modern cowboy crew, smoking is not only *not* universal, it is rather uncommon. Most of the cowboys I have worked with didn't smoke, and of those who did, only one, Sandy Hagar, rolled his own from scratch. If Prince Albert and Bull Durham depended on cowboys for their sales, they would go out of business. Photographers who want to get pictures of the gen-u-wine old-time puncher rolling his own smoke had better hurry, because there aren't many of them left.

But if the tobacco companies have lost sales in the smoking department, they have more than picked up the slack in the chewing department. The use of chewing tobacco and snuff among modern cowboys is almost univer-

A man who shows up on a roundup crew smelling of whiskey does not make any friends.

sal, and for that reason you never want to ride on the down-wind side of a bunch of them. Today's chewing tobacco comes in two forms: plug and loose-leaf. Most brands in either form contain a sweetener that makes the tobacco more palatable. Some brands are quite sweet, others moderately so, and others, such as Tinsley plug, contain little or no sweetener. I know one rancher who uses Tinsley. He's an old-timer, and you rarely see him without a chew. In church, at precisely fifteen minutes before the sermon is supposed to end, he will cut a quid of Tinsely off his plug and slip it into his mouth. I have often wondered what he would do if the spirit moved over the congregation and the service went into overtime.

Most cowboys seem to prefer the sweetened varieties of chewing tobacco, and most seem to prefer loose-leaf over plug. The brands you see most often are Union Standard and Red Man, with Beech-Nut a close third. I am an exception to the general rule because I prefer plug tobacco. My favorite brand is Bloodhound, which says on the label that it's a "dog-gone good chew." I buy Bloodhound by the case (fifteen plugs for eight dollars) and I am never without a plug of it in my shirt or chaps pocket. During roundup season, when everyone's consumption of chewing tobacco soars to an all-time high, I carry a spare plug in my saddlebags and several more in the glove compartment of the pickup. When I need a calling card, I tear the picture of the red bloodhound off my carton and and leave it under the windshield wiper of a friend's pickup. There is never any question about who was there. I am sometimes called "old Bloodhound," and some of my cowboy friends have amused themselves by referring to my brand as "Birddog" or "Hounddog."

The most common form of tobacco used on a modern cowboy crew is snuff, or as it is euphemistically called in the ads, "smokeless tobacco." When I was growing up in the Texas Panhandle, no one but the most disreputable members of the community used snuff. At that time Levi Garrett was the most common brand. It was a brown powder that came in an amber bottle, and kids my age really didn't know what snuff-dippers did with it, whether they chewed it or sniffed it or packed it into their cheeks. We didn't know because nobody around us used it. We considered it daring to smoke and chew, but anybody who dipped snuff would have suffered an erosion of prestige.

Sometime between 1962, when I graduated from high school, and 1971, when I began doing research for a book about the Canadian River valley, the prevailing attitudes about snuff underwent a remarkable change. In 1972 I saw a can of Skoal for the first time. It was in the possession of a young cowboy who worked on a ranch west of Canadian, Texas, and he had been using it long enough so that the hip pocket of his jeans bore an imprint of the little round snuff tin. By that time snuff-dipping had moved into the cowboy crowd, and at this writing it remains the most common vice to be found in ranch country.

Snuff has become quite respectable, and indeed has almost become a badge of honor. But this isn't the same snuff we knew back in the 1950s. The brown powder and amber bottle are gone. Today's snuff is flavored and comes in cheerful little cans, under the brand names Skoal, Happy Days, and Copenhagen. It is not sniffed up the nose, but is placed, a pinch at a time, inside the lower lip. Snuff-dippers can be identified by a distended lip, which becomes very apparent when they try to talk or laugh. Cowboys have various names for snuff. I have heard it called "snoose," "Cope" (short for Copenhagen), and "cud," but most refer to it as just plain snuff. I have never heard a cowboy speak of it as "smokeless tobacco," which may indicate that the advertising campaign featuring football star Walt Garrison has failed to sanitize the nomenclature.

Pranks are almost as much a part of the modern cowboy's life as chewing tobacco and snuff. Sometimes they are simple and harmless. Other times they are elaborate and can amount to a rough brand of play. A cowboy who worked on a ranch in the Canadian River valley had a habit of falling asleep on his horse, and his companions gleefully exploited this weakness and spent hours dreaming up new pranks to play on him. Once they led his horse under a tree with a low branch that swept him out of the saddle. Another time they let him ride ahead of them, then they all galloped forward, yelling and screaming as they rode past, and left the poor fellow in possession of a bucking bronc. Another time they led his horse into a deep pond.

Jake Parker of Beaver, Oklahoma, told me about an elaborate prank he witnessed. A branding crew of about ten men was moving from one pasture to another. Their horses were loaded in two stock trailers, and the cowboys piled into the back of the pickups. One of the boys on this crew—we'll call him Charlie—was a nice, quiet fellow who didn't think too quickly. Charlie was riding in the first pickup, but his horse was in the trailer pulled behind the second. The boys in the second pickup got together and hatched a plot. They stopped, unloaded Charlie's horse, and turned his saddle around backward. When they reached their destination, all the cowboys jumped out and ran for their horses, yelling, "There's a coyote! Let's chase him!" They leaped on their horses and rode away, while Charlie tried to figure out why he couldn't mount his backward saddle.

Cowboys have a lively sense of humor and are always pranking. You walk up behind a fellow in a branding pen and step on his spurs so that he can't move. You sneak around to someone's horse and take the loop out of his catch rope, so that when he needs to rope a calf, he's shooting blanks. You tie the sleeves of his jacket into knots. If a man is standing in a branding pen and is preoccupied with something, you run up behind him and yell, "Watch the bull!" You tie a tin can to the back of his stock trailer so that when he starts home, he'll think a wheel bearing is going out. You ride up behind a man's horse, grab the horse's tail, dally up to the horn, and ride off. There is no end to the pranks cowboys will play on each other, and that is one of the things that make working with them so enjoyable—as long as you keep your eyes open and don't let a couple of yea-hoos ride up behind you with a rope stretched between their horses. If they get that rope under your horse's tail, it's rodeo time.

Hollywood movies and television westerns have created the impression that whiskey and cowboys are constant companions. In her book *The Last Cowboy,* Jane Kramer adds to this impression. Kramer spent some time on a ranch in the Texas Panhandle, and if we believe what she says in the book, the cowboys she encountered were never more than two steps away from a bottle of bourbon. If her main character, Henry Blanton, is indeed the *last* cowboy, you get the feeling that he will succumb, not to agribusiness and modern technology, but to cirrhosis of the liver.

Maybe I've lived a sheltered life, but my observations of cowboys and whiskey are very similar to those made by Philip Ashton Rollins fifty years ago: "The cowboy had to earn his living, and he knew that in the long run wages and alcohol were inconsistent" (*The Cowboy,* p. 188). I can only recall a few occasions when I smelled whiskey on a cowboy during working hours. They weren't drunk or even close to being drunk, yet I stayed as far away from them as I could. I have heard tales about cowboys who went out with a pint in their saddlebags or boot tops, but I have never observed this.

A cowboy in the Texas Panhandle.

What I have seen is that cowboys are strict prohibitionists during business hours. They don't preach it and they're not the least bit pious about it. They simply know that whiskey dulls the reaction time, gives a man a false sense of courage, leads to sloppy work, and can get somebody hurt. A man who shows up on a roundup crew smelling of whiskey does not make any friends. Drinking on the job is regarded as a sign of weakness and a lapse of professional standards. If he wants to drink on his own time, that's his business. But if he drinks while working, he weakens the team and takes chances with the lives of other men.

Just as I have never seen a drunken cowboy on the job, I have never seen two cowboys fight on the job. Many cowboys could certainly be regarded as potential brawlers. Certain elements are present in them that would make them more likely to fight than men in other, milder professions. They are physical men, they have a simple code of right and wrong, and they are prone to take matters into their own hands. Yet maybe these characteristics themselves act as a deterrent. Cowboys tend to respect one another. They don't crowd or push the other man or invade his physical space. They know which men can't take a prank or a teasing, and they leave them alone. They know which men have short tempers, and they stay out of their way. Working cowboys have some taste for action and violence, but they get enough of both in dealing with horses and cattle. Whatever poisons they carry in their systems are vented through their work, and their relationships with other cowboys are peaceful and harmonious.

When a young fellow in boots and a big hat is booked at the county jail for brawling, you can almost bet and give odds that he doesn't work full-time on a ranch. If he did, he'd probably be home in bed.

Since cowboys work long hours and usually live out in the country, their recreation is often closely related to their work. On a Sunday afternoon a cowboy might take his boy down to a fishing hole on the creek. He might work with a young horse, do leather work, or practice heading and heeling in the nearest roping arena. But there is another form of recreation that he pursues all the time, even when he's on the job: he plays with language. The good, natural cowboy humorist makes up his language as he goes along, twisting it into odd shapes that can be delightful and highly descriptive. To the basic information and dry facts, he adds embellishment, exaggeration, and extravagant comparisons, and makes the simple act of talking a pastime and a form of entertainment. I have spent many pleasant hours listening to cowboys talk, and I would like to offer a few examples that I have collected over the years.

Here is an example of a perfectly outrageous response to a simple question. I had a cowboy friend on the Beaver River. His wife had gone to visit relatives and he had been baching for a week. I stopped by one day to see how he was getting along. "How's the bachelor life treating you?" I asked him.

"Oh, it ain't bad," he said in his slow drawl. "But last night the sink got so full of dirty dishes, I had to pee outside."

As expressions of contempt, how about these: "He ain't worth eight eggs." And, "I'd like to buy him for what he's worth and sell him for what he thinks he's worth." And, "He had license to be pretty sorry."

Here's a cowboy's description of his spendthrift son: "If you put a dollar bill in one pocket and a wildcat in the other, I don't know which one would get out first."

And here is something an ornery old cowboy told my four-year-old son: "Most folks smell with their noses and run with their feet. But I was made backwards. My feet smell and my nose runs."

Here is a cowboy's comment on the state of the economy: "If you see a rabbit and no one is chasing him, times ain't too bad."

A cowboy, bragging about his horse: "He can pen a rooster in a stovepipe in a four-section pasture." Another cowboy, bragging about his: "He'll run a cow down a prairie-dog hole and paw the ground till she comes out."

A cowboy complaining about his horse: "You couldn't get him out of a walk if you tied a rake to his tail."

On the dry weather: "It would take forty acres to rust a nail."

A cowboy describing his boss's reaction to a big repair bill: "He squealed like a pig under a gate."

This fellow has been accused of stretching the truth. To defend himself, he replies, "If I say a chicken dips snuff, you'd better check under his wing for a can of Skoal."

I heard a cowboy say this to a companion who was slow to join in some hard work: "What are you gonna do, sit on the bank and watch the crawdads die?"

Here is an aphorism. I haven't quite figured out what it means, but it sounds good: "You can walk with a wooden leg, but you can't see with a glass eye."

A tired cowboy, commenting on a string of long days in the saddle: "We haven't wrinkled the sheets much this week."

At the kitchen table, a newly married cowboy makes a crack about his wife's cooking. His friend, who is older and wiser in the ways of women, leans over and whispers, "You'd better watch that kind of talk, or you'll be wearing that chair for a necktie."

Sandy Hagar on the YL Ranch in Oklahoma was one of those men who built and invented language. He rolled his own Prince Albert cigarettes, which he called "hot tamales." A cigarette butt was a "snipe," and when he ran out of P.A. he poked through the ashtray and went "snipe hunting." In his vernacular, chewing tobacco was "ambir," baby food was "grow-pup," and a man whose name he couldn't remember became "Pete Endgate" instead of Joe Blow. He listened to the weather report on the "radiator," and on a hot day he cooled off in front of the "air commissioner."

Here is a gem of cowboy understatement which was much admired and passed around by cowboys in the Oklahoma Panhandle. A cowboy got bucked off his horse and had to go to a chiropractor to get his neck straightened out. He hobbled into the office and the doctor asked him what on earth had happened. The cowboy was too proud to admit that he had been planted in a sandhill, so he said, "Well, my horse went down and stepped on my hat."

The doctor frowned. "Stepped on your hat?"

"Yalp. My head was in it."

My favorite example of cowboy understatement comes from the Wolf Creek country south of Perryton, Texas. Late one night a cowboy was driving home to the ranch, perhaps with a few beers under his belt. He fell asleep at the wheel and rammed his pickup into a bridge abutment. The pickup spun around several times and came to rest out in the pasture. Bleeding and battered, the cowboy walked to the nearest house and hammered on the door until he roused the neighbors out of bed. The rancher opened the door and stared at the injured man on the porch.

"My god, Jim, what happened!"

"Aw," the cowboy looked at his feet, "muh pickup quit on me."

6

A Day in the Life

This is Saturday, and four or five members of the local roping club are out practicing.

It is mid-April. We have stopped feeding the cattle and spring roundup season is coming up. We need to run a few errands in town before we get too busy with the spring work. But before we go, we must take care of some chores.

We leave the house around eight and walk fifty yards to the barn. This ranch has a good set of working corrals beside the barn. They are made of steel landing mats and creosote-dipped posts, with a two-by-six board running along the top. There are six pens in the corral, four of them connected to a central alley. At shipping time, the cowboys will use the alley for sorting cows and calves. Then we will put all the calves in one pen, drive them into the loading chute, and load them into cattle trucks. That job will come in October. Right now, the pens are empty.

We walk to the barn and open the sliding doors on the south and whistle for the horses, who are grazing out in the horse trap, a small pasture of fifty acres that lies west of the barn. Through the locust trees, we see one horse raise his head and look at us. Then he starts plodding toward the barn. The other horses follow. We go inside the barn and open the doors on five feed stalls, and as the horses come inside, we close each door as a horse enters a stall. We give each one a coffee can full of rolled oats.

56

While they are eating we go into the saddle room, a dark eight-by-ten room with cement walls and floor. This is where we keep our saddles, bridles, bits, spurs, chaps, pads, and ropes. Last fall, we shot a deer and left him hanging from the rafters in the saddle room all winter. When we needed some venison we cut off steaks with a pocket knife and kept the carcass wrapped in a sheet. We finished off the deer in February.

Since we're not rushing off to a roundup or feeding cattle this morning, we have a little time to oil our saddle and tack. In the saddle room we take down a gallon can of neat's-foot oil and pour about a quart of it into a coffee can. We get a soft cotton rag, dab it into the oil, and run it all over our saddle, which is sitting on a wooden rack. The cinch leather seems a little stiff, so we dip it into the oil so that it will get a good soaking. If we didn't keep it well oiled, it would soon stiffen up with horse sweat and deteriorate. We check the dally rubber on the saddle horn. It's getting worn, so we fetch an old inner tube out of the cabinet, cut off four strips about one inch wide, and wrap the horn with fresh rubber. We use the dally method of roping, and we know that dallying is much easier when you have good soft rubber on your horn.

We check the front cinch webbing and see that two strands are broken and another one is frayed. We'd better pick up a new one in town.

We take our shotgun chaps off the peg on the wall and give them a thorough soaking with oil. Leather dries out quickly in the dry Panhandle climate. We are proud of these chaps and we want to keep them soft and pliable. Next, we oil our bridle reins, head stall, and spur straps.

By this time the horses have finished eating. We go into the barn with a halter and lead rope, lead a horse outside, and tie him to a post. Then we get our hoof-trimming tools (nippers, rasp, and hoof pick) and go to work. This is a backbreaking job, and we don't enjoy doing it, but when we join the other cowboys on the roundup crew, we don't want anyone to think we don't take care of our horses' feet. We trim and rasp, trim and rasp, until all five horses have gotten their spring manicure and we have gotten an aching back. We didn't do a beautiful job of trimming. A professional farrier would have done much better, but he would have charged twelve bucks a head.

We turn the horses out into the pasture, close up the barn and saddle room, and walk to the machine shed, a long shelter made of poles and corrugated tin which gives the ranch machinery some protection from the weather. Under this shed we keep the pickup, stock trailer, a small Ford tractor, which we use for digging postholes, clearing snow, and maintaining ranch roads, the cattle sprayer, which is mounted on a small two-wheel trailer, and a lot of junk that just seems to end up here: old tires, gunny sacks, soda pop bottles, and baling wire. We start the pickup and drive around to the gas tank beside the feed barn. While the tank is filling, we step inside the feed barn and take a quick inventory of feed. We rough-count about five tons of 32 percent protein feed left over from the winter.

Next, we drive up to the boss's house and ask if he needs anything from town. We make up a list of items we need: laying mash for the hens, windmill leathers, three hundred doses of three-way vaccine, which we will use at the spring branding, and a case of Quaker State thirty-weight oil.

At last we're ready to make the drive into town. We cross the cattleguard north of headquarters and drive west on the sandy road that follows the river. In the summertime the sand gets dry and deep, and if you're not careful you can get yourself stuck. We pass a big wild plum thicket and notice that it is covered with white blooms. If we have a good year, some Sunday afternoon in July we'll gather two or three bushels of plums and make them into

A day in the life of a cowboy can be made miserable by the weather, as it was here. Tom Ellzey and I found ourselves gathering cattle in a muddy field, when the temperature was thirty-three degrees and a cold rain was falling.

jelly. Wild plums make the finest jelly in the world.

Half an hour later we cross the Clear Creek bridge and see the town of Beaver, four or five miles to the west. It's a pretty little town of about two thousand people, built on the gentle hills south of the Beaver River. In the 1880s it was nothing but a rest stop on the old Jones and Plummer Trail, a trade route over which merchants from Dodge City, Kansas, freighted supplies to the buffalo range in the eastern Texas Panhandle and then carried hides back to the railhead. Later, the town became a supply point for ranches along the river. Today, it retains the flavor of a sleepy cow town, though it has enjoyed a little burst of prosperity and population growth stimulated by the discovery of oil and natural gas in the area.

We stop at an intersection at the south edge of town, directly across from the rodeo arena. This is Saturday, and four or five members of the local roping club are out practicing. The club buys Corriente steers out of Mexico, and members gather at the arena two or three days a week to practice heading and heeling. Beaver has produced some fine team ropers, and many of them compete in jackpot ropings and amateur rodeos during the summer months. Some of them make enough money to pay their expenses, and some don't. Most of them get into team roping just for the fun of it, because they enjoy working with horses and take pride in their roping skills.

We turn right on Douglas Avenue and drive to the north end of town, where we back up to the loading dock at the feed store. Inside, we joke with Big John and Eddie and throw ten sacks of laying mash into the back of the pickup. Then we drive two blocks to the central business district and find a place to park. We go into the drugstore and buy a case of chewing tobacco. Once the roundup work begins, we might not make it back to town for a month, and we sure don't want to run out of Bloodhound.

Then we walk across the street to the saddle and boot shop. This is our favorite store in Beaver, and it's the favorite stop of every cowboy in the area. Lloyd and Bessie stock a good selection of tack and Nocona boots, and Lloyd keeps all the local cowboys well shod, patching and half-soling their old boots until he can talk them into buying a new pair. Bessie makes chaps to order, from the colorful batwings that the rodeo boys like to wear, to the more subdued shotguns of the ranch cowboys. You can go in and choose your style and leather, let Bessie take your measurements, and in a week or two you'll have a new pair of chaps that fit like a glove.

We go inside and start browsing. We glance at three new Tex-tan saddles, shiver at the prices, and move on to the south wall. Here, we look at Trammel bits, spurs, bridle reins, halters, hackamores, bosals, tie-downs, quirts, lead ropes, headstalls, curb straps, breast straps, roping cinches, saddle pads, and latigos. Geeze, if a cowboy had some money, he'd go crazy in this place! We look at four different styles of front-cinch webbing and select one that sells for ten dollars. We lay it down on the counter and move on over to the rope display.

Lloyd has the best selection of ropes in the area, and you just can't walk out of the store without swinging a few of them. If you're a head or horn roper, he's got soft-lay nylons, braided nylons, grass ropes, and the new poly ropes. If you're a heeler, he's got four or five different varieties of heel ropes, each with a slightly different feel to it. He even carries a thin, light nylon rope that is made especially for little boys who want to rope with their daddies. We play with several ropes and walk away, quickly, before we are seized by a sudden impulse to buy one of them. Last time we were in Lloyd's place, we walked out with a new medium-lay nylon. We've got three ropes at home, and that's enough.

We wander over to the boot display, one whole wall stacked high with new, mellow-smelling Nocona boots. We look at a black elk-hide boot with a stacked heel and a high top. Then we look at an elephant-print cowhide boot that has some nice stitching on the leg. We ask the price. "Ninety-five bucks, and they're going up next month." We try them on. They fit, they feel very good. Our balance at the bank is $23.65. We've got to get out of here!

We pay for the cinch webbing and flee. Out on the street we take a deep breath and cast one last glance through the front window. "Boy, if a guy just had some money . . . ."

Our next stop is the hardware store. We buy a case of Quaker State oil and two boxes of graphite-treated windmill leathers. We remember that we also need a tail spring for an eight-foot Dempster windmill. Terry gets down his big Dempster parts book and finds the number, then we go to the back of the store and rummage around in the bins of windmill parts until we find the right spring.

It's twelve noon, time for lunch, so we drive down the street to the cafe. This is the only eating place in town (others have bloomed, only to wilt and fade), and it is always full at the noon hour. Everyone comes here to eat: lawyers, truck drivers, oil field hands, bankers, business people, and cowboys. We sit down at the counter, order a chicken-fried steak, and strike up a conversation with a member of the local roping club. He works at a job in town and keeps his horse on a little patch of grass south of the city limits. He's a heeler, and we've seen him rope at the rodeo. When he leaves the box, he's swinging a small to medium-sized loop, but as he moves in for his throw, he feeds the rope and increases the size of his noose. By the time he makes his throw he has a huge loop that wraps around the steer's hocks and usually comes up with something.

We talk about roping. He went to Dodge City, Kansas, last weekend and won two hundred dollars. When he got back home he had to spend three hundred repairing his pickup. His wife is beginning to wonder if they can afford his bad habit.

Another fellow joins us at the counter. He's young, just out of high school. He works at odd jobs around town, and during the summer he follows the amateur rodeo circuit. He rides bareback broncs, and we've heard that he's pretty good. He'll probably rodeo another year or two, then get married and take a steady job. Like many young rodeo hands, he has never worked on a ranch. Rodeo began as an extension of ranch work, but as the years pass the connection between the two becomes more remote.

We finish off our steak, banana pudding, and iced tea, pay the check, and get on with our business. We drive out to the veterinary hospital to get the three-way vaccine. The vet is working on a Hereford cow with a prolapsed uterus. We watch him push the womb back in and stitch the cow up. He washes his hands in the sink and gets a carton of Cutter three-way vaccine out of a cabinet. We chat for a while about the weather and the cattle market, and agree that only God knows what either one is likely to do. We climb into the pickup and start back to the ranch.

We drive down the wide main street, and just this side of the Beaver River bridge we throw one last glance back at the town. It's a nice little town, and we always enjoy coming in for a few hours. But when the time comes, we're always ready to leave and get back to the sandhills and sagebrush and the slow rhythms of the animals.

PART TWO: TOOLS OF THE TRADE

7

The Horse

There are many kinds of horses, and over the centuries they have been used in many different ways: war horses, hunting horses, jumping horses, draft horses, coach horses, circus horses; horses for track racing, polo, rodeo, and show; and some nothing but pets. There are Italian breeds, Polish breeds, Persian, Mongolian, African, and American breeds, and breeds from virtually every corner of the globe where the horse has been used. Horses come in various sizes, colors, and temperaments. And for every breed and every use, there is a body of theory and a school of riding. The American ranch horse is only one member of a very large family.

The first ranch horses in the West were descended from the mustang, which was brought to the New World by Spanish explorers, escaped, multiplied, and ran wild. Old-timers in Texas and Oklahoma have told me that these early cow horses tended to be small by modern standards, perhaps because of centuries of inbreeding or poor nutrition, or because horses with any size were hitched to a plow. Depending on who is telling the story, you can hear that these early ranch horses were inferior to modern breeds, or that they were superior in every way. My own guess is that the quality of ranch horses has improved in modern times.

Once ranchers had established themselves in the West and had enjoyed a

Doc, cutting-horse stallion on the Three Cross Ranch in the Oklahoma Panhandle.

Three weaned colts. It will be three or four years before they are trained and broke and ready to earn their wages on a ranch.

few years of prosperity, they began upgrading their horse herds by bringing in breeding stock from the outside. On today's modern ranch you will find a smattering of paints, pintos, palominos, thoroughbreds, Appaloosas, and Arabians, but by and large the general service horse in the West is the American quarter horse. Well adapted to ranch work, the quarter horse has good speed over short distances and a gentle disposition, and his powerful shoulders and hindquarters give him the size and strength you need in a ranch horse. Over the years, certain sires and bloodlines have produced horses of demonstrated ability in cutting, roping, and other areas, and many cowboys are amateur scholars on the subject of horse genealogy. They may read nothing else, but they devour every issue of the *Quarter Horse Journal* and the *Western Horseman,* and they can tell you which bloodlines are most highly prized at the moment. Perhaps the most respected line of quarter horses today goes back to a stallion named Three Bars. If you ride a Three Bars horse, it is understood that you are well mounted, and it sometimes appears that *every* horse for sale in the West has Three Bars breeding. As a cowboy once remarked to me, "Hell, two-thirds of the horses and half the fence posts in this country came out of Three Bars."

In rodeo and related sporting events, horses develop highly specialized skills and are rarely used for anything else. There are calf-roping horses, steer-roping horses, barrel-racing horses, heeling horses, bulldogging horses, and cutting horses, and while these animals are often held up as models of what a horse should be, I am inclined to believe that a good arena horse is not the same as a good ranch horse. An arena horse earns his keep by doing one particular job extremely well, yet he may not be adept at other forms of work. A good ranch horse (in my humble opinion, you understand) should be a generalist rather than a specialist, and he should be able to perform any one of a dozen different skills.

What is the perfect ranch horse? First, he is big and stout, yet he should not be so ponderous that he can't put in a long day's work in rough terrain. He should have a gentle disposition, but should still have enough spirit and vinegar to respond immediately to the nudge of spurs or a command to "get up." He should have a good "handle" so that he turns and stops without a struggle. He should have a thick skin so that he doesn't gall easily, and strong feet and ankles that are not prone to injury. He should have the reactions and agility of a cutting horse. He should have all the qualities of a roping horse: enough speed to catch a calf, enough size to drag a grown cow into a trailer, enough training to keep the rope tight when the rider has dismounted, and enough good sense to keep from getting himself tangled up in the rope. He should be smart enough to avoid holes and to wallow through water and quicksand, and calm when he finds himself in situations he has never experienced before. And finally, he should be a good keeper, able to stay sleek and fat on a simple diet.

I have never met this horse and I don't know any cowboy who has. What you find in ranch horses is what you find in mortal men: varying degrees of imperfection, with occasional bursts of magnificence. No single horse can turn in an excellent performance in all areas of ranch work, simply because the physical qualities required in one area preclude competence in some other area. Size and endurance are good examples of this rule. The big, stout quarter horse that can pull a house down simply cannot be expected to carry his bulk around the pasture and stay up with the little Arabian, which was bred for endurance, and the Arabian, for all its endurance, cannot be expected to drag and manhandle grown stock at the end of a rope.

Cowboys always dream of the perfect horse but never find him, and that is one reason they keep a string of several work horses. With several horses to choose from, they can select the one that best suits a particular job.

Some ranches maintain their own breeding stock and raise all their own horses. They may keep a band of brood mares and breed them to selected outside stallions with preferred bloodlines, in which case the mares will have to be transported to the stallions and the rancher will have to pay a stud fee, which may be as little as one hundred dollars or as much as twenty-five hundred dollars or more in the case of well-known and highly publicized stallions. Or the ranch may keep both mares and stallions and do all the breeding on the place.

The major advantage of having a breeding herd is that all the working stock is raised, broke, and trained on the ranch, which means that the history, breeding, and temperament of every horse is known and that the training of the animals reflects the wishes of the rancher. Through close supervision and careful culling, the rancher should be able to mount himself and his cowboys on the kind of horses he thinks are right for his type of operation. If he ends up with knotheads and broncs, he has no one to blame but himself.

But there are disadvantages, too. Maintaining a breeding herd of horses is expensive. Not only do you have the initial expense of breeding animals (and good breeding stock is never cheap), but you must have enough pasture to run mares through the summer and you must keep them well fed through the winter. If you keep stallions, you must have a good set of stud pens. Stallions cannot be run in the same pasture with geldings or other stallions, since they are bad about fighting and running other horses through fences. Nor can they be kept across the fence from geldings or other stallions, for the same reason. One stallion can be run in a pasture with several mares, but most often stud horses are kept in a stout pen, and when mares

Most male ranch horses are gelded (castrated) before they reach the age of two years, because a gelding has a more pleasant disposition than a stallion. Here, a crew of cowboys on the LZ Ranch in Texas throw a young horse with soft cotton ropes, so that he can be gelded. It's a big job that requires a lot of manpower.

need to be bred, they are brought to the stud. To put it bluntly, stallions are a nuisance. They require constant care and supervision, and if kept in a stud pen, they must be fed every bite of grain and hay they eat.

And then there are the veterinary bills. Common old ranch horses that run on grass all their lives never seem to require the services of a vet. The horses that get cut, injured, and sick, and the mares that have trouble foaling, are the high-powered, expensive breeding stock. Because they are valuable property, you tend to fuss over them and attend to their every cough and limp, and often this means calling in a professional veterinarian. Vet bills add up and can be a major expense.

You must also add in time and labor. Someone has to care for and feed the horses, someone has to watch the mares when they are foaling, someone has to record the cycles of the mares and breed them when they come in season, and someone has to keep all the feet trimmed, the manes roached, the tails free of tangles and burs, and all the coats brushed. Foals must be broke to lead, colts must be broke to ride, and young horses must be ridden and trained. If a ranch keeps eight brood mares and breeds them every year, that means that at any given time there will be twenty-four young horses on the ranch, ranging from foals to green-broke colts, with which someone must work on a fairly regular basis. And that is no small chore.

Because of the expense, labor, and facilities required in a horse-breeding operation, many ranchers don't keep breeding stock at all and buy all their horseflesh from the outside. They would argue that you can buy a horse cheaper than you can raise one. The rancher, or whoever is in charge of purchasing, might attend the periodic horse sales at livestock auctions in the area and look over the offering. This is a risky way of buying horses, since there are many ways of making a bad horse look good in a sale ring, and you never know exactly what you have bought until several days after the deal is made. Or he may attend the annual sale at a horse farm, in which case he will have time to look over the animals and check on their papers and breeding before they go up for sale. Here, the buyer can rely on the reputation of the farm to assist him in making his choices, but he will have to pay a premium price for anything he buys.

Or he may deal with the local horse trader. Some horse traders have a lurid reputation, but there are good ones around who perform a valuable service. They know horseflesh and are familiar with virtually every saddlehorse in the country. They are constantly buying, selling, trading, testing, and training horses, and when a customer comes to them wanting a particular kind of horse, they either have one that will fit the description or they know where to find it. The good horse trader works with a regular clientele and he knows that his best interests lie in making a good match. He has as much integrity as you have a right to expect in a horse trader, which is to say that every horse has its flaws and that the trader may not feel obliged to list every flaw of every horse to a buyer who ought to be smart enough to figure things out for himself.

The rancher or cowboy who deals through a reputable horse trader can buy mature horses that are ready to go to work, which means that he saves himself the time and expense of breaking and training colts and maintaining costly facilities and breeding stock. If he doesn't particularly enjoy training horses, or if he doesn't have the patience and temperament for it, this is probably the best solution. He will have to pay a commission, but if the horse trader makes a good match, it is worth the money.

On some ranches, breaking and training horses is part of the cowboy's job. Since the horse is the most important tool on a ranch, bringing young horses along is an important task. Good tools make every job easier; poor tools make every job more difficult.

There are many approaches to horse breaking. In the days of the Old West the procedure was short and not so sweet: a cowboy climbed on a raw horse, spurred him into submission, and rode him until he quit bucking. He was then a "broke" horse and went on to receive on-the-job training. Today, the cowboy has more time to spend with a colt, and the breaking-training process often begins when the horse is young. Instead of climbing on his back and running some iron into his shoulders, the cowboy will spend months handling a colt, gentling him down, building up his trust, and gradually working toward the day when he climbs into the saddle for the first time.

Jake Parker, my old cowboy friend from Beaver County, used to say that there were a lot of sorry horses in the world, and most of them were made sorry by the men who broke them. He believed that a man imposed the flaws of his own character onto a horse, and when he saw them and had to live with them every day, he cursed the horse. Only his associates knew that he was cursing himself.

Over the years I've ridden many horses, some good and some bad. I have browsed through articles and books on horse breaking and studied the methods of other cowboys and ranchers. I have broken a few horses myself. I don't pretend to be an expert on horse breaking and training, but I've given it a lot of thought. It seems to me that the theory is fairly simple. If you start off with a young horse that has not been soured either through genetics or improper handling, you should approach him in the same way you would approach your own children. In other words, the same general rules that apply to child-rearing work well on young horses.

In both areas the objective is not conquest, but rather growth and education. You begin by recognizing and respecting the integrity of the other party. A child develops his own unique personality at an early age, and so does a colt. Within this personality are the strengths and weaknesses of the individual. Over a period of months and years, you try to nourish the strengths and to minimize the weaknesses. You establish rules of behavior and follow them in a consistent manner. When your colt transgresses the rules, he must know that he will be punished, and that the punishment will fit the offense. When he does well, he should be praised and rewarded. You must always remind yourself that a colt is young and likely to make mistakes. You must allow him to make mistakes. You must remember his limitations: he gets tired, he gets bored, he gets angry. You must assume that he wants to learn and to please you, and you must be willing to communicate with him on his own level. After all, *you* are supposed to be the older, smarter party in the relationship, so it is your obligation to find out how to talk to the colt.

This approach to horse breaking requires a great deal of time and patience, and I suppose a lot of cowboys would snort at my ideas, saying that if you're too nice to a horse, you pamper him and make him into a pet. I don't think so. To me, it's a matter of common sense that what you put into a horse is what you will get out of him. If you give him time and patience, you will be rewarded with a good horse—a good, honest, functional tool that will try to please you and give you everything he has. If you attack him and try to conquer him, you will get a horse that doesn't like you, doesn't want to please you, and, like a rebellious child, will find ways to make your life unpleasant.

Every horseman has his own ideas about the qualities he wants in a finished horse, and what one man chooses to ride every day, another would not tolerate. The two qualities I prize most highly in a horse are a soft mouth and an even disposition. By ''soft mouth'' I mean that the horse handles easily; you can stop him and turn him without getting into a wrestling match. An even disposition might mean several things: he is calm and friendly; he is eager to please; and he enjoys ranch work. The importance of this last point was brought to my attention by Jake Parker, who observed that a lot of "sorry" ranch horses do not enjoy cow work. They have learned through experience that when they get around cattle, the fellow on their back is sticking them with spurs, cursing, jerking the bit, and slapping their ears.

It seems to me that if, after the early stages of breaking and training, you have a young horse with a good mouth and a good disposition, you have a solid foundation on which to build the other qualities you want in a ranch horse, whether that be cutting, roping, or whatever. The horse will pick them up with time and experience.

These rules will not apply to every horse, and I don't know of any that will. Some horses will not allow you to use gentle methods. In my book *Panhandle Cowboy,* I tell about a mare named Gypsy, a half-thoroughbred whom I tried to break when she was six years old. I tried to be gentle and patient with her, only to discover that she was not going to be gentle with me. It takes two to tango, and if the horse is not willing to accept discipline and training, then the cowboy has no choice but to use sterner measures. Gypsy and I had a turbulent relationship, and we had many sessions that were direct confrontations of will. She didn't like me and I didn't like her. We fought for two years and I finally gave up, reasoning that if I gave her enough time, she would eventually hurt me badly or kill me. I hated to admit defeat, but it seemed the wiser choice.

When a cowboy takes a job on a ranch, one of the first questions he must settle involves his string of work horses: will he ride horses belonging to the ranch, or will he furnish his own? Some cowboys keep one or more horses of their own and take them wherever they go. Others don't have personal horses, and they have no choice but to ride company stock.

On the surface, it appears that the cowboy is better off using ranch horses. This saves him the expense of buying his own working stock (and right now, you can figure on spending a thousand-dollar bill on any decent ranch horse), and heads off potentially troublesome questions about compensation: is the ranch going to pay him for the use of his personal horse (probably not), and will the ranch compensate him for the horse if it is killed or crippled in the line of duty? The cowboy could easily take the position that he isn't going to furnish working stock for the ranch, tie up his own money, and use his horse to do the ranch work, when the chances are that he won't be paid for it.

That's a sound argument, but there's another side to it. The cowboy is a kind of craftsman, and like any craftsman, he depends on good tools. A horse is his most important tool. If he rides ranch stock, he is using someone else's tools. The ranch horses might be well broke and trained, or they might be complete jugheads. If they are, then his job will be more difficult. On the other hand, if he owns a horse and has spent several years working with him, then he has at least one mount that can get the job done. Even if he doesn't get paid for the use of his horse, he will have the satisfaction of going to work a-horseback instead of a-foot (poorly mounted).

He might also consider this matter strictly in terms of his own self-interest. Why should he break and train another man's horses when he could be breaking and training his own? The more a horse is ridden, the better he becomes and the more he is worth. A cowboy might spend two years riding a colt that belongs to the ranch. Just when he gets the horse about where he wants him, the boss comes along and says, "A feller bid me fifteen hundred for old Button, and I just can't turn him down." The horse is sold, the rancher pockets the money, and the cowboy is back to riding colts again. In effect, he has functioned as a horse trainer and has increased the value of another man's property. Maybe he'll get a bonus or a commission. Maybe he won't. A wise old cowboy once gave me this piece of advice. "Ride your own horses and improve your own stock. Then, when you leave this ranch and move on to another, you'll have something to show for your time. 'Cause when you leave here, they ain't going to give you any more than a good-bye kiss."

8

Pickups and Trailers

Stock trailers have revolutionized the cattle business in just a few years.

There was a time in the Old West when a cowboy did just about everything a-horseback. The modern cowboy still does much of his work a-horseback, but he has also come to depend heavily on two very useful pieces of equipment: the pickup and the stock trailer. Used together with a horse, they have vastly increased his range and mobility, and they have given him the mechanized tools that allow him to look after more country and do a better job.

Pickups and light trucks have been around almost as long as cars have, but from what I have gathered from old-timers, they did not make much of an impact on ranching until after World War II. During the war, American automakers learned how to make a light truck that could travel in the sands of North Africa, the snows of Russia, and the rocky terrain of Italy, and when this technology was brought home and applied to civilian vehicles, it led to the production of pickups and light trucks that could get around in rough country and take the constant pounding and abuse of ranch work. By 1950 most cowboys had parked their mules and wagons and were making their winter feed runs in some sort of motorized vehicle, either an army surplus jeep or a civilian copy of it.

Stock trailers did not appear in large numbers until about ten years later.

A three-quarter-ton, four-wheel-drive pickup equipped with a feed box. The box is loaded with pelleted feed and equipped with an electric auger. The driver can string out cake on the feed ground or into troughs without stopping or handling sacks. It is a handy device for the cowboy who has a lot of cattle to feed in the winter.

This is the best cowboy rig I ever ran across. The pickup is a three-quarter-ton, four-wheel-drive vehicle, equipped with an electric winch on the front and a two-way radio. The stock trailer is small (fourteen feet by five feet) and highly mobile, and it is well suited for loading roped cattle in the pasture.

When I was working on the Flowers Ranch in the late 1950s, we had a small two-horse trailer and a bobtail truck, but no stock trailer. We had never heard of such a thing, and as far as I know, stock trailers simply didn't exist. Then, during the 1960s, they came on the market, and by the time I returned to ranching in 1970, stock trailers were everywhere. Every farmer and rancher owned one and pulled it behind his pickup, and he probably wondered how he had ever operated his business without it.

The primary difference between a horse trailer and a stock trailer lies in size and capacity. A horse trailer, usually divided into two or four compartments, allows the owner to transport horses over long distances, and for years it has been popular among rodeo cowboys, horse breeders, and people who attend horse shows. The horse trailer was an improvement over the earliest horse-hauling apparatus—a pickup with stock racks around the bed—but it was too small to be used for any large-scale hauling of cattle.

Then in the 1960s someone came up with the idea of making a trailer that was large enough to haul cattle, and which could also serve the function of the horse trailer. By that time pickups had enough power to pull such a trailer, and all at once stock-trailer factories were springing up all over the country, and farmers and ranchers were standing in line to buy the trailers. It was an idea whose time had come. The cattleman could do all his light hauling with the stock trailer and combine the functions of two pieces of equipment: the horse trailer and the bobtail truck.

Today, the use of stock trailers in ranch country is almost universal, and if you walk around the parking lot of a livestock auction, you will see an amazing variety of pickup-trailer rigs. Each one fits the particular needs of the owner. The stockman who doesn't need to haul large numbers of cattle or horses will probably own the basic, bread-and-butter type of trailer. It will

This is a good cattle-hauling rig. The twenty-four-foot gooseneck trailer is pulled by a three-quarter-ton flat-bed pickup with dual rear wheels.

be five or six feet wide, fourteen to sixteen feet long, and it will have a center gate that divides the inside space into two compartments. It may be covered from front to back with a roof made of metal or canvas, or it may be open. This type of trailer hitches to the bumper of a pickup, and it can be pulled by an ordinary half-ton pickup.

From here, the trailers get bigger and more exotic, and so do the pickups that pull them. The big trailers are all "goose-necks," which means that the hitch attaches to a ball or fifth wheel in the bed of the pickup. The bumper hitch is all right for small loads, but for heavier loads it is unsatisfactory. A heavy load pressing down on the back bumper of a pickup lowers the back end, raises the front, and can make the pickup unstable and dangerous to drive. The goose-neck hitch places the weight of the trailer directly over the back wheels of the pickup, where the shocks and springs are stout enough to support it, and the goose-neck pulls smoothly down the road. The big goose-necks may be thirty feet long and eight feet wide, have six wheels instead of four, and come equipped with electric brakes that are coordinated with the brakes of the pickup. The man who pulls a big goose-neck might be a cattle buyer, a horse trader, a yearling operator who is constantly shifting cattle around from one pasture to another, or a rancher who needs the big goose-neck to transport cowboys and horses from one place to another.

Big trailers require big pickups. A half-ton pickup can handle the standard bumper-hitch trailer or a small gooseneck, but it would soon fall to pieces if it had to pull a big trailer loaded with cattle. That is why you see the big goose-necks hooked up to three-quarter-ton pickups, three-quarter-ton flatbeds, one-ton flatbeds, and three-quarter-ton "dualies"—pickups with dual rear wheels which are specially designed for pulling trailers. The biggest pickup-trailer rig I ever saw was a real monster, and in fact it was nothing but a small semi-truck. The trailer had an upper and lower deck, and it was pulled by a short-wheel-base truck similar to those that are used to pull mobile homes on the highway.

What the working cowboy needs in a pickup-trailer rig is not the same as what a cattle buyer needs, and in our country the typical cowboy rig consists of a half-ton or three-quarter-ton pickup hitched up to a sixteen-by-six-foot trailer. This gives the cowboy the capacity to haul small numbers of cattle, but hauling cattle is not the primary function of his rig. Most of the time he uses his trailer for transporting his horse from headquarters to outlying pastures. In the standard stock trailer, he can haul up to four horses, or he can put cattle in one compartment and horses in the other. What the cowboy needs in his trailer is not size but mobility.

The best cowboy rig I ever saw was one I used when I worked on a ranch on the Beaver River in the Oklahoma Panhandle. This cow-calf operation consisted of winter pastures along the river near headquarters and several outlying summer pastures up on the flats, from eight to fifteen miles from home. I did most of my driving in this isolated country over pasture trails and dirt roads, and I needed a rig that could travel through mud, snow, and deep sand.

For this, I had a Ford F-250 high-axle, four-wheel drive, three-quarter-ton pickup, with a four-speed transmission and a V-8 engine. (The three-quarter-ton pickup is bigger and made of heavier material than a half-ton. The axles and springs are more similar to those of a truck than to those of a car.) Four-wheel drive was not a luxury on this ranch, but a necessity. Even in fair weather I could hardly drive around the ranch without using the four-wheel drive once or twice to get through sand, and in wet or snowy weather I stayed in four-wheel drive all the time.

Around the bed of the pickup and behind the cab, I had a set of heavy "headache racks" made of welded pipe. On these racks I could hang various tools that I needed in my work: posthole diggers, shovel, a hammer, several chains, fence stretchers, booster cables, and a lariat rope. On the front bumper I had an electric winch that ran off the battery. I could use the winch for stretching up fence, pulling old posts out of the ground, or pulling someone out of a mudhole. By bolting an A-frame gin pole into the front bumper, I had enough vertical lift to pull pipe out of a windmill and hoist heavy objects.

This pickup was also equipped with a two-way radio that gave me a communication link with three base stations and eight mobile units on three ranches along the river. In this rough and isolated country communication was difficult, and the radio was not only handy but rather comforting at times. I didn't use it a great deal, but it was nice to know that if I ever needed help, I could raise someone on the radio.

The pickup was a rugged, functional piece of machinery, and so was the trailer. It was quite ordinary in appearance; it wasn't big, it wasn't flashy, it wasn't even pretty. What you saw at first glance was a faded fifteen-by-five-foot bumper-hitch trailer with a fabric cover over the front compartment. The beauty of it appeared only to the man who used it every day. It was simple, durable, and very mobile. I could jump my horse inside, throw the pickup into four-wheel drive, and reach any corner of the ranch in any kind of weather.

But the feature which appealed most to me, and which was invisible to everyone else, was that it was a perfect tool for pasture roping. This is the second function of the modern cowboy's stock trailer: its use as a portable corral and catch pen.

This sequence demonstrates the use of horse and rig in loading an animal out in the pasture. I hauled my mare to a pasture where we had a stray heifer. In the first shot, I'm driving the heifer toward the trailer. Since I use the dally method I am driving her on a loose rope—neither tied nor dallied to the saddle horn as long as she cooperates. Next, I am dragging her up to the trailer parked on an incline so the back and middle gates hang open.

In the last shot, while the heifer catches her breath, I flip my rope over one of the hitch balls welded to the top of the stock racks on the left side of the trailer. The next step is to drag her inside and shut the gate.

Let's say that during the summer months we find a cow in the pasture with an advanced case of cancer-eye, a common malady in adult Hereford cattle. A good herd manager watches for cancer-eye all the time and detects it in the eye of a cow when it is little more than a white "tick" the size of a navy bean. Sometimes these ticks will remain dormant for years, but other times they will spread rapidly over a period of two or three months and will reduce the eye to a grotesque bloody mass. If the cow is not sold, she will eventually die. A cow with a mild case of cancer-eye can be sold as a packer cow, which means that she will go to a packing house and will be made into hamburger, lunch meat, and such. A cow with a bad case of cancer-eye will not pass inspection and cannot be made into meat products. Instead, she will be rendered into by-products (tallow, glue, pet food), and her salvage value at the time of sale will only be half that of a healthy animal. Hence, part of good herd management lies in spotting the bad-eyed cows and getting them to a livestock auction before they lose their salvage value.

We've spotted a bad-eyed cow in the pasture, and we've decided that she has to go to town. But this summer pasture does not have a good set of corrals. If it did, we could just drive the cow into the pens, load her into the trailer, and head for town. Without corrals, we have to load her in a more primitive manner: rope her and drag her into the trailer.

She weighs about nine hundred pounds, so we choose a big, stout horse for the job. We load him into the trailer and off we go to the pasture. We find the cattle down by the windmill and spot the bad-eyed cow. We memorize her markings in case the cattle scatter and we have to pick her out on the run. We ride toward the cow and ease her out of the bunch, since we don't want to frighten and scatter the whole herd when the chase begins. She leaves the herd and breaks into a run. We fall in behind her. If she isn't too fast, we may get a good shot right away, and with a little luck we will fit the noose on her neck on the first throw.

When the loop drops over her neck, we dally to the horn and bring her to a stop. She struggles at the end of the rope for a minute or two and discovers that she has been captured. When she settles down, we ride around behind her and drive her toward the trailer. Horses that are exceptionally strong and good pullers can drag a grown cow a short distance, but it's always better to drive the critter if she will drive.

We drive her to a point about fifty feet from the back end of the trailer, and there she stops. We drag her toward the trailer gate, moving down the left side of the trailer. (A left-handed roper would work from the other side.)

Before we rode out for the cow, we parked the trailer on a slight incline, facing uphill, so that when the back and center gates were unlatched, they would fall open and stay open. And we studied the wind direction to be sure that a strong gust of wind wouldn't blow them shut. In other words, we left the trailer open and ready to receive the cow.

We've dragged her to a point about six feet behind the open rear gate. She has choked down and is more concerned about getting her wind than escaping. That's what we want, because in order to move on to the next step in this maneuver, we must have the cow temporarily immobilized. While she's catching her breath, we slacken the rope, ride up to the middle of the trailer on the left side, flip the rope over a hitch ball that is welded to the top of the stock racks, dally up to the horn, and ride forward, pulling her toward the trailer.

This is a crucial point. If the horse is stout and if the cow stays on her feet, it can be over in a matter of seconds, with the cow stepping up into the trailer. But if the horse is not a good puller, or if the cow falls down before she gets her front feet into the trailer, it can drag on for half an hour. When she steps into the trailer, we close the rear gate, crowd her up to the front compartment, and close the center gate behind her. Then we fish the rope off her neck with a shovel handle, load our horse into the back compartment, and head for town.

Loading grown stock in this manner is a hard job for one man, but with this particular stock trailer it's about as easy as it can be, because of the way the trailer was built and designed. The rear half of the trailer is not covered, which means that you can come in and flip your rope over the stock racks and go right to work. If the entire trailer were covered, you would have to run your rope into the trailer, under the roof, and through the side. This is difficult for one man to do, and if the cow is fighting, it is almost impossible. There is a way of doing it, but it requires the use of a second rope, a well-trained horse, and considerable luck and patience. The hitch balls welded to the top of the racks make the job much easier and give the cowboy leverage on the rope and just the right pulling angle he needs. These balls are made of heavy steel and are smooth all the way around, so that they don't have any sharp edges that will cut up a rope. They did not come with the trailer, but were the invention of some unnamed cowboy who had dragged enough stock into a trailer to figure out how to make the job easier.

Stock trailers have revolutionized the cattle business in just a few years. The modern cowboy crew has the mobility of a motorized army, and the roundup boss who has thoroughly studied the matter of logistics can dispatch his men to different points in a big pasture, or split the crew and send half to one pasture and half to another. If the pickups are equipped with CB or two-way radios (and many are), he can even make last-minute refinements in his strategy and maintain radio contact with cowboys four or five miles away. This allows him to gain maximum use of his crew, to cover a lot of country in a short period of time, and, in the process, to save the horseflesh for the primary tasks of rounding up and sorting.

Stock trailers also have allowed cattlemen to expand their operations into seasonal grazing programs. Cattle that are summered on ranch grass can be moved in the fall to stalk fields and wheat fields, in which they will remain until green grass comes again in the spring. If the distance between the ranch and wheat pasture is not too great, the rancher can haul the cattle himself in stock trailers. And during the winter, if cattle stray or get sick, he can throw a horse into his trailer and attend to the problem. This kind of seasonal grazing would be difficult or impossible without the mobility provided by the stock trailer.

There is a hidden weakness in the mobility of the modern cowboy: it is based upon the use of petroleum energy. A pickup that pulls a loaded stock trailer burns a lot of gasoline, and if the price of gasoline continues to rise, the time may come when cattlemen will have to sacrifice mobility for economy. If that day comes—and I suspect that it will—we will see fewer stock trailers and more cattle drives, and the cattle business will be changed from top to bottom.

9

Pasture Roping, Then and Now

The cowboys who subscribed to one method of roping viewed cowboys of the other school with amusement and even contempt.

The lariat rope is a tool of the cowboy's trade with which he can perform a number of specialized functions. Of all the skills a cowboy possesses, roping is the one he prizes most highly and the one most intimately linked with the glamorous and romantic side of the cattle business.

A cowboy may draw substandard wages, and in town he may be regarded as a mere hired hand. He may have patches on his blue jeans and holes in his socks, and he may drive a rattletrap car whose muffler is tied up with baling wire. But when he's a-horseback, when he holds a rope in his hands, when, with a flick of his wrist and a flip of the rope, he can bring an animal weighing half a ton to its knees—that cowboy may be a common man, but he doesn't feel like one.

On the surface, the catch rope is nothing but a glorified piece of clothesline. It doesn't require fuel, oil, or grease. It won't rust if left out in the rain. It has no cogs, gears, wires, tubes, or transistors. It doesn't have to be sharpened or cleaned. It is perhaps the simplest tool ever devised by man.

But of course it isn't quite that simple. Each skill and profession tends to develop a technology and a specialized language, and the deeper you probe into the skill, the more complicated it becomes. That is true of roping. Not all ropes are the same, and not all ropers use the same style. Roping equipment and styles have changed a great deal since the cattle business began a little more than a century ago.

The first ropes in the New World were the braided rawhide reatas of the Mexican vaqueros, which saw use in California and parts of the Southwest where Mexican cowboys were employed. The vaquero had his own special style of roping, and he raised it to an art form. When he caught a critter, he dallied the rope around the saddle horn. (The word *dally* is a corruption of the Spanish term *dale vuelta,* which meant "give it a turn." In the mouths of American cowboys, this became "dolly welter" or "dally welter," and finally just plain "dally.") The primary reason the Mexican cowboy dallied his rope was that his rawhide reata was not stout enough to take a strong jerk and would break if an animal was brought to a sudden stop.

The old-time reata ropers did not rope for speed and did not jerk cattle around. Once they made a catch, they dallied up to their horns and played the animal as an angler might play a big fish on a light line. They carried a long rope of sixty to eighty feet and rode saddles with a single rigging (only one cinch around the horse's middle) and a horn covered with rawhide that was designed for taking the turns of a rope.

I once heard a West Coast cowboy talking about the reata ropers he worked with in California years ago. They were all of Mexican extraction, and they were expert in the use of their rawhide ropes. In a branding pen they often necked calves at a distance of thirty or forty feet. When a good reata roper wanted to show off in an exhibition, he would let his rope slip around the horn until smoke began to rise from it.

The reata style of roping flourished in places where two types of people could be found: Mexican cowboys who knew how to use the reata, and craftsmen, usually Mexican, who knew how to braid them. But as the cattle industry moved north into the Great Plains region, and as cowboys moved farther away from the influence of Mexico, roping styles and equipment began to change. Cowboys in the Texas Panhandle, Indian Territory, Kansas, and Montana didn't know how to braid rawhide ropes and couldn't afford to buy them even if they were available. These prairie cowboys adopted the grass rope as their own, and they developed their own style of using it.

The grass rope could take a jerk better than a reata, and since American cowboys were more prone to be in a hurry than their Mexican counterparts, they were more inclined to bust an ornery critter than to play with him until he wore down. They had no patience with the dally approach, and they began tying the home end of their ropes "hard and fast", dispensing with all that foolishness of winding the rope around the horn and coddling cattle. Prairie cowboys tied solid and rode a double-rig saddle (one with a front cinch, plus a back, or roping, cinch).

It would be a mistake to say that prairie cowboys were unaware of the dally method or that they never used it. I have seen a Charlie Russell painting that showed a Montana cowboy using a form of the dally; he has wound his rope around a small, slick horn and is pinching the two pieces of the rope together to make the dally hold. More recently, artist Jack Bryant has done a painting called *Stuck in the Mud*, which shows a modern cowboy using the same technique to pull a cow out of a bog.

From time to time, prairie cowboys found it necessary and wise to untie the horn knot and go to the dally. But their use of the dally was occasional and unsystematic. They had not trained themselves in the art of handling cattle on a loose rope, which involved controlling the coils in the left hand, controlling the slack with the right, and taking a lightning-fast dally when the roped animal tried to run away. And while their saddlehorns functioned well for holding a figure-eight knot, they were poorly designed for dally roping—too short, too narrow, and too slick. When prairie cowboys dallied, they did it crudely and with improper equipment. Their use of the dally was a variation on the hard-and-fast method, not part of a larger system of roping.

The cowboys who subscribed to one method of roping viewed cowboys of the other school with amusement and even contempt. The dally ropers felt that the hard-and-fast boys were little more than circus performers. They had speed but no style. The hard-and-fast cowboys replied that the dally men were so preoccupied with style that they never got any work done.

Feelings ran high on both sides. In his book *Trail Dust and Saddle Leather,* Jo Mora, a reata man to the marrow of his bones, recalled that when he first drifted into California around 1900, it was "almost a felony on the statute books" for a man to be seen riding a double-rig saddle and tying hard and fast to the horn. In *A Thousand Miles of Mustangin',* Ben K. Green, a Texas cowboy who firmly believed in tying solid to the horn, gave his low opinion of the dally method: "I never wrapped and dallied and gave slack when ropin' stock. That's the way to lose fingers in the rope and that's the way to get your hands rope burned and lose what you've caught, and damn a coward, if you haven't got nerve enough and confidence in your mount to double half-hitch and hard tie, you are going to scar up your hands and lose more stock than you keep" (p. 18). It is odd that Doc Green, and many other prairie cowboys who tied solid, associated dally roping with a lack of courage. It is odder still that in *Wild Cow Tales,* old Doc admitted to using the safer dally method when he roped a wild cow (p. 50) and a wild mule (p. 58).

These were the two primary styles of roping used by the old-time

A rope tied hard and fast to the horn.

punchers. But what about the modern cowboy? What style does he use, where did it come from, and in what ways is it different from the methods used by the old-timers?

The modern ranch cowboy has developed a roping style out in the pasture that draws something from both of the old-time methods, but which is new and unique in other respects. Taking a close look at his saddle, the first thing we notice is that he carries neither a rawhide reata nor a grass rope, but rather a rope made of nylon. The second thing we notice is that his nylon is not tied solid to the horn. The third thing we see is that his horn is wrapped with strips of inner tube, a sure indication that it has been prepared to take the wraps of a dally. I can't speak for other parts of the country, but in the Texas and Oklahoma Panhandles where I have worked with cowboy crews, these observations hold true 90 percent of the time. You rarely see a grass rope these days, and almost never do you see the home end tied to the horn. Most of the cowboys I know have gone to the nylon and to the dally.

There isn't much mystery about why they have gone to nylon ropes. Nylon is stronger and more durable than grass, the loop holds its shape better, and the rope doesn't stiffen up when it is exposed to water or cold weather. To put it simply, most modern cowboys believe that the nylon is a better tool than the grass rope.

I have wondered why cowboys in the prairie states decided to go to the dally method, because it is more difficult to dally-rope than to rope hard and fast. When you're tied solid, you make your toss, flip the rope to keep your horse from stepping over it, and then slow or stop him to tighten the noose on the animal's neck. That's pretty simple. But when you dally, you're handling a loose rope, which means that you can't just stop your horse; you must keep him running and maneuvering until you take your wraps around the horn. And the dally technique is complex. When you stick your loop on the critter's neck, you reach for your slack with your thumb pointing back at you, pull the slack to tighten the noose, bring the rope back to the saddlehorn, and give it a counter-clockwise turn, keeping your thumb pointing upward.

Proper technique is very important in dally roping, because if you dally incorrectly or carelessly, you might get a finger or thumb cut off in the rope. That's why you want to have your thumb pointing upward when you take your wraps. Ben Green, who railed against the dally method, just didn't know how to do it right. He probably dallied upside down and backward, and I would imagine that he was trying to take his wraps on a small, slick saddlehorn that was designed specifically for holding a knot, not for taking a dally. If Doc had troubled himself to learn the proper technique, and if he had used a saddle with a bigger horn, wrapped with strips of rubber or soft leather to increase its holding power, he might have had a better opinion of dally roping.

So why did cowboys on the Great Plains change to the dally technique when it is harder to dally-rope than to rope hard and fast? I have put this question to several cowboys who were old enough to have started out roping in the hard-and-fast days, but who later learned to dally and now use the dally method all the time out in the pasture. It was their opinion that dally roping moved eastward out of California, that it first appeared in the prairie states in the 1950s, and that working cowboys learned to dally in the arena and then took it home to the ranch. In other words, ranch cowboys learned to dally, not by watching other ranch cowboys, but by watching pros and semipros roping in the arena.

Jake Parker, foreman of the Three Cross Ranch in the Oklahoma

A rope dallied to the horn. The horn has been wrapped with strips of inner tube to increase the friction between horn and rope. The roper's left hand holds the coils, while his right hand is in the proper thumb-up position.

Panhandle and a consistent one-loop roper out in the pasture, explained it this way: "When I was growing up, nobody dallied. Everybody carried a grass rope and tied it to the horn. I can remember the first dally roping I ever saw in Beaver (Oklahoma) in the fifties. The local boys were trying to dally for the first time, and they were slow and awkward. They dallied upside down and backward. The dally method was new, and they hadn't learned how to do it.

"I think the dally came into use in team roping after the first time dally ropers competed against hard-and-fast ropers at the National Finals Rodeo. The dally ropers beat the tar out of the knot boys, and if you stop and think about it, you can see why. A header who knows how to dally is a lot faster than a header who's tied hard-and-fast. The dally roper only has to deal with fifteen or twenty feet of slack, and if he's good, he can dally on half his rope and get the steer turned in a hurry. The hard-and-fast man has to let the steer go the full thirty feet, and then there is some danger that he'll trip him before the heeler gets there." (Erickson, "Pasture Roping over the Years, Part 1," pp. 48–56)

By the time the dally method had moved into the Great Plains and had been adopted by arena ropers, it had undergone many changes. Gone were the rawhide reata, the sixty-foot rope, and the emphasis on style rather than speed, which were the trademarks of the vaquero. What the arena ropers did was to take the two old-time methods of roping, blend and modify them, and come out with a new, distinct style of roping. But surely there must be other reasons why ranch cowboys have gone from the knot to the dally, something besides the fact that dally roping happens to be in style. My guess is that when the nylon rope came into widespread use, cowboys became aware of the hazards of the hard-and-fast method. The old-time cowboy who roped a heavy animal with a three-eights-inch grass rope could get himself out of a storm by riding hard away from the critter and breaking his rope. Nylon changed all of that. The superior strength of a nylon rope is an advantage until you want to get divorced from whatever it is you've put your string on, and then it becomes a marriage contract. If you're tied solid with a nylon rope, the fine print says that the contract is binding "till death do us part." If you're dallied in a storm, you can turn loose of the rope and ride off. It may cost you a new rope, but ropes are still cheaper than coffins.

The typical cowboy of the old days, the one who tied solid to the horn and would put his twine on anything that walked, tended to be young, single, and perhaps something of a rakehell. Today's cowboy is likely to be older, and in most instances he has a wife and family at home. If he can find a way of increasing his margin of safety out in the pasture, he is inclined to do so. He is astute enough to realize that the dally method is the cheapest form of health and life insurance a cowboy can find.

And there may be one last factor that helps explain the increasing use of the dally: it is easier on cattle. The cowboy who handles a loose rope is keenly aware of the possibility that he might miss his dally—and get his hand scorched by a hot rope, and then have to chase it around the pasture for an hour or so to get it back. With this in mind, he is not nearly as prone to throw trips on cattle or to stand them on their heads, and hence he is not nearly as likely to break legs and necks as his old-time counterpart who was tied solid. In a time when cattle are worth some money, this advantage of the dally method cannot be ignored.

The roping techniques used by working ranch cowboys have changed a great deal over the past century as each generation has faced a different set of circumstances and has adapted its use of the rope to its own particular needs. The work routine and ranch conditions of the modern cowboy are not the same as those of his old-time counterpart, so the way the modern puncher uses his rope is not the same as the way the old-time puncher used his.

To understand the evolution of roping styles and techniques, we must sketch a brief history of ranching and place the working cowboy in a historical context, since to a large degree this context has determined how and when he has used his rope. In this discussion we will deal only with ranching in the Great Plains region and will not consider the reata school of roping that flourished on the West Coast.

We might call the first historical period the Golden Age of roping. It began after the Civil War with the maverick hunters in South Texas and included the cowboys who worked the big free-range outfits. The old trail drivers also belonged to this period, as did the punchers who worked the big fenced-range outfits up to about 1930. What all these cowboys had in common was that they lived and worked in an era when fenced pastures and working corrals either did not exist or were extremely rare. The importance of that fact to the history of roping is obvious. When a cowboy had to catch a horse, he roped it out of a remuda. When he needed to give a cow critter some special attention, he had to rope it first. A cowboy during that period had to know how to use his twine, and one single loop or roping style would not serve all his needs, so he was forced to master several.

In his book *The Cowboy at Work*, Fay Ward gives an excellent and detailed account of roping styles used during that period. He observes that the old-time puncher generally employed six different roping techniques, each one designed for a specific job. When he was a-foot in a corral and wanted to neck a horse, he threw the pitch catch. This loop was not rotated over the head but thrown out to the side and directly from the starting position. The horizontal loop was pitched with one rapid motion at the animal. If the man wished to fore-foot a horse, then he threw the slip catch, in which the loop was carried behind the roper and tossed vertically in front of a running horse.

The hoolihan was a more versatile loop, since it could be used on the ground for catching horses out of a remuda or on horseback for necking calves in a branding pen. To deliver the hoolihan, the cowboy made one clockwise swing over his head and turned the loop over so that the honda (eye of the rope) was on the right instead of the left side. The two advantages of the hoolihan were that it was a quiet throw that did not frighten animals in a corral and that since the honda naturally traveled down the rope the loop closed quickly. However, under most conditions it was not suited for pasture roping.

For pasture roping, the cowboy employed three techniques. The first, of course, was the standard overhead catch, which he used to neck-rope everything from baby calves to grown stuff. When he came up against horned animals, he modified his technique to pick up the horns, throwing his rope so that it would sweep in from right to left instead of falling over the animal's head. In *Wild Cow Tales*, Ben Green tells of a third variation of the standard head shot in which the critter is caught around the head and over one horn so that the loop tightens down on the animal's windpipe and chokes him down.

The second pasture loop was the heel shot, used in team roping when another cowboy had caught a critter by the head or horns. Fay Ward's description of the old-time heeling technique depicts the cowboy holding the loop shoulder high, rotating it with his wrist, and swinging it vertically out to his side. Modern heelers tend to throw a horizontal loop that comes in flat and wraps around the animal's hocks. They use both wrist and elbow movement and must concentrate on keeping the elbow up.

The third pasture loop employed by the old-time cowboy was the one he used on heavy animals, bunch-quitters, and outlaws, and which probably did more to give ropers a bad reputation than all the other loops combined: the forefooting catch. This loop was thrown over the shoulder of a running animal in such a manner that it caught both front legs. When the catch was made and the cowboy turned his horse at a sharp angle, the result was, as one old-timer described it, *buenas noches* for the cow brute. At the very least, the critter took a hard fall, and often he never got up again.

The old-time cowboy had to know how to put his twine on an animal out on the open range, but that was only the beginning. If he worked alone, and he often did, he also had to know how to get his rope back. To accomplish that feat on grown animals that were sometimes eager to fight, he had to develop techniques for throwing animals to the ground and temporarily immobilizing them. He did it by throwing trips and busting them. In the early days of the cattle business, it was a necessary and essential part of the work. But you get the impression that young cowboys who tied hard and fast and rode swift ponies developed a taste for busting cattle and turned pasture roping into a form of entertainment. The result of such abuse was predictable: broken legs and broken necks in the cow herd, and an unhappy boss at headquarters. Ropers developed an unsavory reputation, and the lariat rope came to be regarded as a crippler and killer of cattle. Indeed, there was an old saying that buzzards followed a cowboy around the pasture, knowing that sooner or later they would get a free meal.

By the third decade of the twentieth century, ranching had made great strides toward becoming an efficient, well-managed business enterprise.

When Jake Parker and I found this bloated heifer on wheat pasture, we headed and heeled her, then put the head rope on her front feet and stretched her out on the ground. While Buck (shown here) and Calipso kept the ropes tight, Jake ran a rubber hose down her guzzle and into her stomach. This allowed the trapped gas to escape.

Roping in a branding pen, Lawrence Ellzey is about to deliver a hoolihan shot at an unbranded calf. While most heading throws are made after several counterclockwise twirls of the noose, the hoolihan throw follows one quick clockwise twirl. It is an excellent technique for corral roping.

Blooded cattle had replaced the old longhorn, railroads had put the trail drivers out of business, the big ranches had been split up, fenced, and crossfenced. As ranchers built shipping pens, working pens, and doctoring chutes, the lariat rope was eclipsed as a ranch tool and roping skills entered into a period of decline. Many ranchers and ranch managers who had seen the roping abuses of the early days issued stern guidelines on the use of the rope, and some, J. Frank Dobie's father among them, did not allow any roping whatever. If a critter needed attention, they said, it could be brought to the house.

During this Dark Age period, roughly between 1930 and 1955, the roping skills of the average cowboy declined and many of the old-time techniques were forgotten. An Oklahoma cowboy who was a lad in the 1930s described it this way: "When I was a kid, there was nobody around who could even hit the ground with a rope. If a man carried a rope at all, it was a limber grass rag that wouldn't hold a loop and had five figure-eights in it. In those days, when a man had to rope something, he ran it down and dropped the loop over its head. There was no skill to it at all. They didn't have good ropes and their horses were ignorant" (Erickson, "Pasture Roping over the Years, Part 2," pp. 106–8).

During this period, ranch cowboys did not rope enough to become highly skilled or to train their horses. Then, when they were forced to rope something, they often ran it to death or got themselves into a wreck because they didn't know what they were doing, which naturally added to the bad reputation of ropes and ropers. There seemed to be no escape from the cycle, and it appeared that ranch roping was headed toward extinction.

Roping skills were saved, not on the ranch, but in the arena. By about 1955, when team roping became popular in the prairie states, ranch cowboys had access to horse trailers and could haul a horse into town on Sunday afternoon. And though it sounds strange, they went to town to learn how to rope. They weren't playing with the boss's cattle now, and they could rope as long as they could lift their arms and pay the stock fee. In the arena they got what they never could have gotten on the ranch—hours and hours of roping practice and access to the modern, scientific methods of roping that had been developed by professional ropers. They were introduced to nylon ropes and to new and better kinds of equipment. They trained their horses. They learned the art of dally roping, and they learned how to handle big cattle. They learned how and when to rope, and when they returned to the ranches, they took these new skills with them.

Of course not all ranch operations followed this pattern. On some outfits, especially the large ones, roping never did go into a dark age. Cowboys continued to use the rope and the old-time techniques have prevailed to the present day, changed little or not at all by the innovations developed by arena ropers. On these ranches you can still find cowboys who know how to throat-latch a horse out of a remuda and who tie hard and fast to the horn.

Spike Van Cleve, a rancher from Big Timber, Montana, has maintained a strong roping tradition on his ranch, as did his father and grandfather before him. He still ties solid to the horn ("If it's worth catchin', it's worth keepin' ".), and Spike has no use at all for the dally—"Because, by God, this is hard-and-fast country, and that's the way it's supposed to be done!"

Is there some way we can compare ropers of the Golden Age with those of the present day and come to some conclusion about which were better? It won't be an easy task, since there is no sure or scientific method of comparing times or degrees of skill. But just for the fun of it, let's try, using common sense instead of a stopwatch.

Here is an example of the method used in tailing down an animal that has been roped by the heels. Billy Nowlin has a double hand grip on the tail, while Tom and Nathan Ellzey are ready on the rope. When they pull in opposite directions, the critter will be jerked off his feet. The other end of the rope, of course, is being held by a man on horseback. On the LZ Ranch we use this method for castrating yearling bulls. The four marks on the animal's left hip indicate that he has spent four days in the sick pen.

At a pasture roping contest near Amarillo, the head roper has put his string on a fast-running corriente steer, while the heeler stands by for a shot. The horns of contest steers are wrapped to protect them from the burns and jerks of a rope.

If we go back to the books and articles written by the old-time ropers, it becomes clear that the modern cowboy knows a great deal less about what a rope can do than did his counterpart who lived fifty years ago. The old-timer could rope cattle and horses, horns, heads, forefeet, and heels, little stuff and big stuff. And, chances are, he could even do a few spinning tricks with a cotton rope. When we moderns read about Ben Green, Fay Ward, and Will Rogers, and see what they could do with their ropes, we feel ashamed of ourselves and regret that we have lost so much of the art of roping.

So there is our first conclusion: the average ranch cowboy of the Golden Age knew more loops and throws and was a more versatile roper than his modern counterpart. And to that extent, he was better.

But here's the second conclusion: in the specialized areas of heading and heeling, the average ranch cowboy of the present day just might be better. Why? For one thing, the horses are better today than they were in the old days. They are bigger and faster, better bred, better broke, better trained, and better fed. If 50 percent of a roper's success lies in his horseflesh (Will Rogers claimed that the horse was 75 percent of a good run), then it makes sense that if the modern ranch cowboy is better mounted, he is also a better roper. (Remember, we're only talking about heading and heeling.)

For another thing, the modern cowboy has access to a body of scientific roping technique that was not available to the old-timers. He has studied the methods of professional and semiprofessional ropers, who just happen to be the best and fastest headers and heelers the world has ever seen. The modern ranchhand may not go down the road or finish in the money, but he has had the opportunity to observe and imitate the methods of the boys who do. The old-time cowboy picked up his roping techniques wherever he could, often through trial and error. There is no trial and error to modern arena roping. It has become a science.

And finally, the modern cowboy handles cattle more gently than the old-timers did. No doubt this is due in part to the fact that the cattle themselves are more gentle and can be handled more easily and also because the cowboy today knows that they are too derned expensive to be busted and wallowed around. Stock trailers have helped the modern cowboy in this regard. If he needs to doctor a grown cow out in an isolated pasture, he doesn't have to throw trips on her or choke her down. He can drag her into his trailer and do his work while she's inside, or haul her to the house.

There's another reason why modern cowboys handle cattle more gently. Where the old-time puncher was tied solid, the modern cowboy is likely to use the dally style of roping. Say what you want about the advantages of the knot over the dally, it's easier to abuse cattle when you're tied solid. Once you've made your catch, you can bring your horse to a quick stop, and when the cow critter hits the end of that rope, traveling at twenty-five or thirty miles an hour, he will sprout wings, do a half-flip in the air, and hit the ground hard on his back. Or you can flip your rope over his hip, turn your horse hard to the left, and throw a flying trip on him. Either way, you can teach him who's boss, and perhaps break his neck as well. A good, fast dally man can punish cattle just as handily as a hard-and-fast roper, but most ranch cowboys lack the lightning speed on the dally that these methods require and are more interested in keeping all their fingers than teaching cattle a lesson. Their style of roping almost demands that they handle stock gently.

These are just my opinions, and I freely admit that I'm a dally man myself and that I never tie solid to the horn. I'm sure a lot of old-timers won't agree with me, but that's all right. In the end, none of us can make an airtight case. But there is one point that we can all agree on. In the first half of this century, roping skills were following the longhorn steer down the path to extinction. If it hadn't been for the boys in the arena—Toots Mansfield, Ike Rude, Shoat Webster, and others—today's ranch cowboy might be riding around with an empty horn string. And he might not even know why it was put there.

PART THREE: WHAT COWBOYS DO

10

Winter Work

In the early 1880s, when Charles Goodnight and other Texas ranchers began upgrading their beef cattle with purebred British stock (Angus, shorthorns, Herefords), the day of the old longhorn cow had come to an end. Through careful breeding and culling, ranchers were able to develop cattle which produced more beef per live-weight-pound than did the old longhorn. In other words, they realized that they could increase their production of beef by upgrading their animals instead of by increasing the size of their cow herds. The British breeds were efficient in converting grass into beef, and because the basic strategy of ranching is to convert raw material (grass) into finished product (beef) as quickly and efficiently as possible, the British breeds soon pushed the rangy longhorn out of the pasture and into the museum.

But for all their advantages, the British breeds had one major shortcoming: unlike the hardy longhorn, they were not self-sufficient. They required more care and special handling. As long as there was grass in the pasture they did all right, but during periods of prolonged drought or during the winter months when the grass lost its nutritional value, the more highly bred stock had to be fed a protein supplement. Without this protein feed they became thin and could not maintain their body weight, and in this

Feeding cattle in the winter is what is called a steady job.

weakened condition they were vulnerable to blizzards and periods of severe cold. Hence, the coming of improved cattle breeds brought the old-time cowboy a job he never really wanted. When the first frost ended the grass-growing season, he had to park his horse, hitch up the team and wagon, and make his daily feed run until green grass appeared again in the spring.

In the Texas and Oklahoma panhandles, the winter feeding on a cow-calf ranch usually begins between Thanksgiving and December 1, and continues until sometime between April 1 and May 1, though the decisions on when to start and when to stop feeding are determined by the range conditions and the condition of the cattle. In a bad year, the feeding may begin as early as August and continue until June.

Each ranch follows its own feeding philosophy that reflects the particular needs of the ranch and the experience of the ranch owner. Until fairly recent times, the most widely used protein supplement was cottonseed cake, a pelleted ration made of by-products after cotton seeds have been pressed for their oil. Cottonseed cake comes in hundred-pound burlap sacks and yields a nutritional value of 41 percent protein. It is a good protein supplement, and many ranches still use it today.

But cottonseed cake is no longer the only supplement available, and in our country many ranches have gone to other types of feed; in fact, it is rather uncommon to find an outfit that uses only cottonseed. This change has occurred partly because of the high price of cottonseed cake, and partly because some animal nutritionists have suggested that a cow critter doesn't need and can't efficiently utilize a high-protein feed. Many ranchers began experimenting with lower protein feeds, such as 38 percent, 32 percent, 20 percent rations, and even 17 percent alfalfa pellets, and they found that their cattle did just as well. What a rancher decides to use as winter feed is often determined by the market. If he can get a bargain price on 20 percent feed, that's what he will use. If he can get a good price on cottonseed, he'll feed 41 percent. Or he may buy some of both and feed one variety one day and the other variety the next, giving his cattle a ration that has a protein value that is an average of the two.

The cowboy is not often involved in the purchasing of winter feed. That is one of the decisions made by the boss. Whatever ration is laid into the cake house is what he will feed through the winter.

Some ranchers feed hay in addition to sacked feed. Protein supplements satisfy the cow's daily requirement for protein, but they provide little roughage. If the rancher stocks his winter pastures heavily, or if he feels he will run short on grass before the winter is over, then he might decide to begin feeding hay after Christmas, after the first of the year, or when the snow begins to fly. There are many kinds of hay, but in our part of the world the three most common varieties are sorghum hay, alfalfa hay, and prairie hay. Each variety has its own advantages and disadvantages, but the decision on what brand of hay to feed often is determined by price and availability. In any case, the rancher has to make his plans well in advance of his needs and get his hay laid in during the summer growing season, when it is least expensive and most readily available.

During the winter months the cowboy's life revolves around the daily feed run, and all other work is subordinated to the task of getting feed to the cattle. At a certain hour of the morning he backs his pickup up to the cake house and loads the number of sacks he will need. If he is feeding hay, he will drive to the hay lot and load bales. Then he drives out to the first pasture, calls in the cows, counts them, puts out the feed, counts them again, studies the condition of the stock, and drives to the next pasture. After the first week, he

Pickup loaded with sacked feed and prairie hay, and ready for the daily feed run.

has established a schedule and routine which he will follow almost to the minute throughout the winter. He is a creature of habit and so are the cattle. Cattle have a mysterious and accurate sense of time, and if the cows in one pasture are accustomed to being fed at ten o'clock, they will usually be standing on the feed ground at that hour. If the cowboy is early, they will be scattered. If he is late, they will be standing on the feed ground, bawling as if to protest his violation of the routine.

Feeding cattle in the winter is what is called a *steady* job. If the cowboy is sick, nursing an injury, or just tired of the daily routine, that's too bad. He has to make his feed run, and unless he is unable to get out of bed or unless a blizzard is howling outside, he will make his rounds. Feeding is most difficult when the weather is most foul. School children may squeal with delight as big, fluffy flakes of snow pile up outside, but the cowboy will grumble and mutter to himself. He must wear overshoes that by the end of the day seem to weigh thirty pounds apiece as he plods through the snow, and in order to drive from pasture to pasture, he must plow through drifts and pick his way across an expanse of white that hides ruts, holes, ravines, stumps, and other obstacles that can halt or slow his progress. He can't afford to get stuck. He must keep moving.

He is on a treadmill and he can't step off. In the depths of January he may be so bored with the same routine, so tired of wading through mud and snow, so sick and fed-up with the isolation and confinement that he wonders why he ever got into this business. He thinks that if he sees one more cow looking at him with those stupid hungry eyes, he will hang himself with his own lariat rope. Day after day, week after week, it's the same routine: back up to the cake house and load the cake; back up to the hay stack, load up the hay, throw it off, go back for more hay, throw it off, and go back for more.

Feeding alfalfa hay when the temperature was near zero, I put the four-wheel drive into compound and let my four-year-old son steer it while I broke the bales and threw them off.

The horses are hungry, the cows are hungry, the heifers are hungry. There is no end to their appetite. They eat and eat and bawl for more, and tomorrow they must eat again. The cowboy begins to feel that he is throwing bales of hay into a bottomless pit. He can't stop, there's no end to it, why didn't he take a nice job in town?

Though the foregoing would be fairly typical of the winter routine on a cow-calf ranch in the central plains, the routine on a yearling operation, where young cattle are wintered on wheat pasture and stalk fields, would be quite different. The yearling operator does not run breeding stock (cows and bulls), but instead buys weaned or weaning-age calves that weigh between 350 and 500 pounds. He may buy his stocker cattle from a cow-calf ranch, out of a livestock auction, or from an order buyer who specializes in buying and selling light cattle. On a yearling operation the winter work begins in the fall of the year when the cattle business undergoes its annual turnover. The cow-calf ranchers sell their calf crop, and yearling operators buy them as stocker cattle and take them through the winter.

On a yearling operation, the first job of the winter grazing season is to receive fresh cattle and get them "straightened out," which means that they must be nursed through a period of stress during which they are vulnerable to disease. The stress derives from several sources. The calf is taken out of the only environment it has ever known, a grass pasture, and hauled in trucks to another environment. In corrals, sale yards, and cattle trucks, it is exposed to dust and bacteria. If the animal is hauled a long distance, it will go through a period of up to twelve or eighteen hours without feed or water. When it arrives at its new home, its digestive system must begin adjusting immediately to a new diet that does not include momma's milk. Taken together, these factors produce stress in the animal and lower his resistance to disease. The yearling operator keeps a close watch on a fresh set of calves and checks them regularly for signs of pneumonia, scours, diphtheria, and a catchall malady known as shipping fever. When he gets them straightened out, which may take anywhere from a week to a month, he has cleared the first major hurdle in the yearling end of the business.

When a yearling operator buys fall calves, he takes them into some type of winter grazing program. It is possible to winter calves on grass and a feed supplement, but the weight gains are small, and often the calves don't gain weight at all. They merely grow and maintain their body weight through the winter and do not begin gaining until green grass comes in the spring.

For that reason, many yearling operators move their cattle to wheat or oat pastures in the fall of the year and leave them there until spring. Wheat and oats that are planted in the fall grow and remain green through the winter, and under the proper conditions, small or thin cattle can gain rapidly on this type of forage. A calf that goes onto wheat pasture weighing four hundred pounds can easily come off in the spring weighing six hundred. In a good year there is an enormous migration of stocker cattle into the wheat-growing regions of Texas, Oklahoma, and Kansas, and to oat fields along the Brazos River in Texas.

In the Texas Panhandle, the influx of stocker cattle onto the wheat fields begins October or in November, when the wheat has reached several inches in height and the plants have developed a root system that will hold them in the ground when a steer takes a bite off the top. Ten or fifteen years ago, most wheat fields had barbed wire fences around them, and before the yearling man turned his cattle into the wheat, he had to go around the fence and tack it up on the posts, replace old posts with new ones, and splice any broken wires. But that has changed in recent years, and today most wheat fields are only partially fenced or have no fences at all. Neither the land-owners nor the cattlemen who leased wheat pasture wanted to maintain a permanent fence that was used only three or four months out of the year. And, as it turned out, there was a better way of fencing seasonal pastures anyway—with an electric fence.

An electric fence consists of a single strand of smooth galvanized wire stretched between two insulated corner posts and supported at intervals of about sixty feet by small steel posts. Electric fence posts can be driven into the ground with a hammer, and they are equipped with plastic insulators that hold the wire. A fence charger, powered either by a 12-volt car battery or by 110-volt house current, sends a charge of electricity into the fence every one or two seconds. When an animal comes in contact with the fence, he grounds the current and receives a bite of electricity that will discourage him from getting near it again.

Electric fencing is very useful to the yearling operator, and it has several advantages over the standard barbed wire fence. Every part of an electric fence is portable, and it is easily installed and taken up. The yearling man, who leases the grazing rights to winter pasture and does not own the land, can fence off his pastures with electric fence and avoid the expense of maintaining a permanent fence on another man's property. When he leaves, he takes his fence with him. And because electric fence is so easy to put in and take up, he can rotate his pastures to get the maximum use out of each one, grazing out one patch and then moving the cattle to another.

In the winter of 1979–80, I worked for the LZ Ranch, a yearling operation near Perryton, Texas, that ran on wheat pasture. In the fall, when the wheat was ready to graze, we loaded the flatbed pickup with steel posts and wire, headed for the flats, and started putting up electric fence. That fall we must

On a yearling operation, winter work includes stringing out miles of electric fence around wheat and stalk fields. The rolling and unrolling of the galvanized wire is done here with a patented wire rolling machine which sits in the back of a pickup.

have built somewhere between twenty-five and thirty miles of fence, and with three of us on the crew, we could fence a section of wheat (four miles of fence) in about three hours. We could take it down just as quickly with the aid of a patented wire-rolling machine that fit into the bed of the pickup. Powered by a small gasoline motor, this device made quick work of what used to be the most difficult part of electric fencing—rolling up miles of wire. Ten or fifteen years ago, this job was done either by hand or with some sort of homemade contraption. The wire-rolling machine does the job quickly and efficiently, winding up to three miles of smooth wire on one spool.

Once an electric fence is properly installed, it must be maintained. The yearling operator must check it every day or two to make sure that it is still hot. One broken insulator, one place where the wire touches a steel post will knock out the entire fence, and a dead fence will not hold cattle very long. When the yearling man goes out in the morning, he puts his fence tester on the wire. If it shows a dead fence, then he must go around the fence until he finds the spot where it is grounding out.

Once the fence has been put up and the cattle delivered to the wheat pastures, the yearling operation settles into its winter routine. Every day or two the electric fence must be checked and water must be hauled, since most wheat fields do not have windmills or surface water. In cold weather the ice on the tanks must be broken so the cattle can drink, and if snow covers up the wheat the cattle will have to be fed hay until it melts off. During the winter months light cattle must be watched closely, because they are more likely to develop health problems than grown stuff. Scours, bloat, and pneumonia are the most common maladies in light cattle, and they must be attended to before the critter gets "straightened out" for good.

When I worked for the Ellzeys, Tom Ellzey and I rode through the cattle on

When you run yearlings on wheat pasture during the winter months, you don't always have a set of corrals around. So you make your own with portable corral panels, which can be fitted together to form a pen of any size and shape.

In twenty minutes, two cowboys can build a corral out of these portable panels. They lock together and support their own weight, which means that fence posts are not needed. In twenty minutes they can be disassembled, loaded into a stock trailer, and hauled to the next pasture. Portable corrals make it possible for the modern rancher to sort and load his cattle in pastures where permanent corrals do not exist.

wheat at least once a week. We roped all the stock that looked sick, loaded them into a stock trailer, and hauled them down to the ranch, where we could doctor them every day and keep an eye on them. As the wheat began to grow and green up in March, we encountered fewer cases of sickness and more cases of bloat. On lush wheat, cattle sometimes eat so much that their digestive system cannot release the gasses produced by the fermenting wheat, and if they are not taken off it, the bloat will put so much pressure on their heart and lungs that they will die.

In our country, the winter grazing season usually ends around March 15 or April 1, unless the cattleman has made arrangements with the landowner to graze out the wheat (graze-out wheat is not harvested for grain), in which case he might leave his cattle on wheat pasture until June. When the modern yearling operator pulls his cattle off wheat pasture, he is likely to make use of another handy invention that has come along in the last ten years: the portable corral. The portable corral consists of twenty or thirty panels made of lightweight tube steel. The panels are light enough (about sixty pounds each) so that in half an hour, one man can set up a pen that will be big enough and stout enough to hold a hundred or two hundred head of steers. When the cattle are penned, one end of the corral can be adjusted to form a chute, and the cattle are easily loaded into stock trailers. Then the corral can be broken down, loaded into a trailer, and hauled to the next wheat pasture. When the cattle are moved, the crew returns to the field and takes up the electric fence. Like a circus, the modern yearling operation comes and goes and leaves hardly a trace behind.

By this time spring is in the air. The days grow longer and the warm sun has melted away the ice and snow. Cranes and geese begin their northward flight. The sage begins to green up, the wild plum bursts into bloom, the cottonwood trees send out their buds, the cattle shed their winter hair, the horses grow sleek and shiny. The cowboy gets the scent of spring in his nostrils and feels good. Winter is over and spring roundup is coming up. He can park his dad-danged pickup, saddle up his horse, and do the kind of work that a cowboy is supposed to do.

11

Spring Roundup and Branding

The enemy, of course, are the cattle, and sometimes they can be formidable.

In a cowboy's life, the spring branding season is a time of joy and excitement. Gone is the deadening routine of winter, the bleak days, the long nights, the cold hands and feet, the incessant demands of hungry animals, the isolation and loneliness. He puts up with these things because they are part of the job and because, in order to ride on a roundup crew, he must submit to a certain amount of drudgery. If he is a true cowboy to the marrow of his bones, he will walk barefoot through hell in order to claim his place on a spring roundup crew.

The spring work in cow-calf country might begin as early as April 15, reach its peak by mid-May, and then taper off by June 15. It may involve sorting and culling the cow herd and moving cattle to summer pastures, but the primary function of the spring roundup is to brand and work the calves that have been born during the winter. Neighboring ranchers often pool their cowboys into one large crew and move from ranch to ranch, rounding up pastures, sorting the cattle, and branding the calves until the work is done.

Rounding up a big pasture is an adventure, and it resembles a military campaign. The roundup boss, usually the ranch owner or his foreman, is the general. He sets the strategy, thinks through the logistical problems of get-

130

Saddling up in the first light of day.

ting his mobile cavalry (mobile because they use pickups and trailers) where they are needed, and then directs the attack on the enemy. The enemy, of course, are the cattle, and sometimes they can be formidable. Wild cattle will test the speed and endurance of the horses and the intelligence, instincts, and courage of the cowboys. Some cow herds will test the crew several times and give up. Some will go on testing until the last animal is driven into the corral and the gate is shut behind them. And some simply refuse to be gathered. I have tangled with cows that were so wild that you dared not crowd them too closely with a horse, because they would lower their heads and run right over you. They respected neither horse nor man, and about all you could do with them was to call in the "long arm of the cowboy:" pitch a nylon rope around their necks and impose your own brand of law and order. (The reader who wants to learn more about rounding up wild cattle might enjoy my book *Panhandle Cowboy,* which deals with the subject in some detail.)

The process of rounding up or moving cattle might be compared to moving a bead of mercury with your fingers across a flat surface. Cattle respond to the pressure placed on them by mounted cowboys. If you don't push them, they stop. If you want them to move forward, you put pressure on the drag-end. If you want to slow them down, you move cowboys up to the point. If they try to break on the flanks, someone rides in to stop them.

A crew of good, experienced cowboys understand the system and don't need to be told what to do. If they know where the cattle are supposed to go, they can figure out the rest on their own. They don't need to be ordered around or yelled at. In fact, one of the quickest ways to bring a cowboy's blood to a boil is to give him orders he doesn't need, in a tone of voice he doesn't like.

Riding drag on a roundup, the cowboy reaches for his favorite toy and amuses himself by heeling the slow-moving cattle at the rear.

I once knew a cowboy who did some day work on the side. He was helping gather cattle on a big ranch one day, and the owner, who was the least skilled man on the crew, began yelling at him. My friend turned his horse, rode back to headquarters, loaded up, and went home. He didn't ask for his check and he didn't say a word to the owner. Telling me about this experience, he said, "That son of a bitch will never yell at me again." The owner of the ranch didn't know it, but he was lucky that the two of them were separated by a herd of cattle. Otherwise he might have learned a painful lesson about what happens when you stick a spur into the wrong horse.

The cowboy loves roundup work, not only because he is able to use his two favorite tools (horse and rope), but also because he has the opportunity to see and visit with cowboys he hasn't seen all winter. Like him, they have been holed up and isolated through the bleak winter months, and they are full of suppressed cowboy energy, which, when they come together on a roundup day, comes bursting out in the form of yarns, stories, lies, jokes, gossip, pranks, and acts of daring. At a spring roundup, the entire world seems to be fragrant and blooming. The country looks good, the horses look good, and the cowboys are full of vinegar.

Once a pasture has been rounded up, the branding work begins. Many modern outfits have gone to the calf cradle, or working chute, either because the boss believes that it is better than the other methods, or because he doesn't have enough cowboys to work cattle by hand or with a rope. At a chute branding, the cows and bulls will be cut away from the calves, the calves will be crowded into a small pen behind the chute, and one man will work the alley and have a calf waiting when the chute becomes empty. A good alley man doesn't need a hot shot (a battery-powered cattle prod) and doesn't want one, since it keeps the calves stirred up and excited and makes them harder to handle. He may arm himself with a piece of windmill rod, but he can do just as well with his bare hands. Unless the calves are exceptionally large or the crowding pen is poorly designed, he can do a better job by twisting tails and forcing the calves down the alley with his knees and legs.

Once the calf enters the chute, the sides of the chute are compressed, the head gate comes down, and the device is tilted over on its side. One man applies the brand, another castrates the bulls, another dehorns, and another vaccinates and keeps tally. A crew of four is the minimum number for a fast, efficient chute operation, though the work can be done with fewer.

Another method of handling calves at a branding is "wrestling," pronounced "rassling" in these parts. In this kind of operation, the cows and bulls are cut out and the calves are crowded into a small pen. When the irons are hot and everything is ready, two or more crews of "rasslers" will begin throwing the calves to the ground. One man grabs a front leg, the other seizes a hind leg on the same side, and they lift up on the animal and throw him to the ground. If the ranch brands on the left side, they will throw the calf with the left side up, and if the brand goes on the right, they will throw him with the right side up. Once the calf is on the ground, the front-leg man sits astride the calf and controls the front legs, while the hind-leg man will hold the hind legs. If the calf's legs are not controlled, someone may get kicked.

Wrestling calves in a branding pen is a lot of fun, but over a period of days it takes a physical toll on the cowboy crew. Small calves can be worked very easily with this method, but big, strong calves are always hard to take down. By the time two cowboys have thrown a 350-pound calf, they will be huffing and puffing, and they may have been kicked and stepped on. If you work on a team with a rookie who doesn't know how to take down a calf, you can work yourself to a frazzle, and your chances of getting kicked rise with the level of inexperience of your partner.

I have always enjoyed wrestling calves, and I prefer it to the chute method. In wrestling calves you take a certain amount of physical punishment, and you are tired at the end of the day, but you are also learning something, improving your skills, and testing yourself against the strength of animals. It is a challenge. I don't find these elements in a chute operation, where a device made of steel substitutes for human brains and skill. After about thirty minutes of working a chute, I begin to feel that I am in a factory, doing dull, routine work that could be done by anyone. There are times when a chute is a very handy piece of equipment—say, when you have a small crew or when you have to brand a large number of big yearlings. But I don't understand why any rancher who had enough cowboys to work the stock by hand would go to a chute operation and deprive the men of the fun and challenge of wrestling. To me, the difference between the two methods is the difference between work and play. Running calves through a chute is work, wrestling calves is fun. If they both pay the same, I would rather wrestle, take my lumps, and have a good time. But not everyone feels that way about it.

The third method that can be used on branding day is the old-fashioned roping method. Here, the cows are not separated from the calves. Everything stays in one big branding pen, and when the irons are hot, two ropers ride quietly into the herd and begin roping calves and dragging them to the fire. If they are good heelers, they will catch everything by the heels. If they are average heelers, they may only heel the bigger calves and catch the smaller ones by the head, since the smaller stuff is easier to head than to heel. When a heeled animal is brought to the fire, the cowboys on the

Branding equipment. The large object is a branding heater which has taken the place of the old wood branding fire on many modern ranches. Branding irons are laid inside the heater and heated red-hot by a propane fire. From left: two dehorning tubes for small horns; castrating knife; vaccine gun; branding iron; hemostats, used for pulling veins in the heads of large animals when dehorning results in severe bleeding; and, bottom, a dehorning saw.

ground, who are working in pairs, will usually "tail" the calf to the ground: one man grabs the tail and pulls, and his partner on the opposite side grabs the rope and pulls. The calf goes down, the tail man sits on the front legs, while the rope man controls the hind legs and releases the rope.

A calf that has been roped by the head is "flanked" down. A cowboy grabs the rope in one hand and the flank skin in the other, rolls the calf up on his knees, lifts it with his legs and arms, and throws it to the ground. His partner is there immediately to control the back legs before someone gets kicked.

A smooth, well-run roping roundup is something to behold. It is like a symphony of work, and I regard it as one of the highest expressions of the cowboy craft. Every man, from the roper to the man on the branding irons, knows his job and does it well. The work is done quickly, quietly, and efficiently. I don't think there is a better method of working cattle.

Of course there is such a thing as a *bad* roping roundup. I have attended a few of those, and they were wrecks. From this kind of circus, roping and ropers get their bad reputation. Ropers who don't know how to work in a herd or handle cattle in a pen are sloppy and even dangerous. If the cowboys on the ground don't know how to take down a roped animal, they can get themselves hurt. Working around a rope requires some skill, and if the crew does not have the skill, it can turn into a very long day.

The primary jobs at a spring roundup are vaccinating, dehorning, castrating, and branding. There isn't much to say about the vaccinating. Obviously, the purpose of vaccinating animals is to give them immunity to certain bovine diseases. It is done using a vaccinating gun with a short needle, and the shot is usually given under the loose skin below the calf's shoulder.

The branding is also simple and straightforward. The irons are heated either on a wood fire or, more commonly these days, in a branding heater that is fueled by propane. The man on the branding iron alternates his irons, so that one is always heating in the fire, and applies the hot iron to the spot on the calf where the ranch has registered its brand—hip, leg, side, or shoulder, and either on the right or left side. He wants to make a good clean brand that will peel and leave an impression years later. If he doesn't press hard enough on the iron, he will not make a good impression, but if he pushes too hard, he can smudge the brand or break through the skin.

Castrating and dehorning are more complicated, and there are several approaches and schools of thought in each area. Bull calves are castrated for two reasons. First, the rancher does not need them or want them as breeding stock. When he needs herd bulls, he buys them from a purebred stock operation that specializes in raising good, high-performance bulls carefully selected for soundness, conformation, and carcass qualities that yield a high percentage of meat. As the saying goes, if you don't buy bulls that are better than your cows, you're losing money. The second reason bull calves are castrated is that the castrated male, called a steer, has certain physical and behavioral qualities that make it the preferred beef-producing animal. Steer beef is probably what you eat in the steak house, and you should hope that no one ever serves you a bull steak. The longer you chew a piece of bull meat, the bigger it gets.

There are many approaches to "cutting" a bull calf. Sometimes the end of the scrotum, or bag, is cut off, and those who follow this method claim that the wound drains better. Sometimes the end of the bag is split, on the grounds that a steer calf looks better if it has a bag than if it doesn't. It is possible to castrate an animal without cutting the bag at all, with a tool called the Burdizzo, which applies pressure to the outside of the bag and severs the

At a spring branding, the roper drags a heeled calf toward the fire, while a wrestling crew holds another on the ground.

A wrestling crew at work. While one man flanks the calf down, his partner gets control of the back legs before the calf has hit the ground.

While two cowboys hold the calf on the ground, the brander applies a hot iron and the head man goes to work on the horns. In the background is the propane bottle used to heat the irons.

While the "head" man saws off a horn, another cowboy comes in with the vaccine gun.

cords to the testicles. The Burdizzo came into use in the South and Southeast where screwworms were a constant menace any time an open wound appeared on a cow critter, but it has never been widely used in the prairie states. Most ranchers in this region consider it unreliable and complain about the high percentage of "stags" (animals that are not completely castrated and show bullish qualities) that are left by the Burdizzo method.

Once the bag is cut or split, the individual rancher will once again use his own tried and tested methods. Some cut the cords right above the testicle with a knife. Some cut the cords as close to the animal's belly as they can. Sometimes the cords are not cut at all, but are pulled apart, scraped with a knife, or even scraped in two with a thumbnail. Still other ranchers perform the job with a special tool called an emasculator, which cuts the cords and then, when gripped tightly like a pair of pliers, stops the flow of blood to the wound.

If you are working on a branding crew and if you are given the job of castrating, you must understand exactly how the rancher wants it done. Your own personal opinion isn't important. If he splits the bag and pulls the cords, that's the way you do it. Ranchers tend to be very fussy about the way the castrating is done, even though it might appear to an outsider that one method is just as good as another, and indeed, the rancher often does all the castrating himself because he considers it the most important job.

There are also many approaches to the dehorning. Animals are dehorned for various reasons, but I think the most important is that slick-headed animals bring more money than horned animals. Virtually all beef animals, with the exception of breeding cows and bulls, end up in a feedlot, where they are fattened for market. They eat at feed bunks, and horned critters take up more room at a feed bunk than dehorned ones. They will have to be

This is a calf cradle, or squeeze chute, used by some outfits to brand and work calves. The advantage of the cradle over other methods is that the job can be done with three or four men.

"How come you let that pony buck you off this morning?" Kent Courson asks young Kevin Ellzey, who had gotten himself pitched off on roundup morning. The big roundup meal is a time of fun and fellowship, teasing and storytelling. And of course there's always plenty of good grub and gallons of iced tea.

dehorned eventually, and a cattle buyer is willing to pay a higher price for this service since he can get a higher price down the line. If he buys horned animals and dehorns them, he will have to take them through a period when they shrink and lose weight because of the shock of the dehorning.

The most common method of dehorning small calves on a ranch involves the use of a dehorning tube, a steel device with a sharp cutting edge on one end and a wooden handle on the other. Using the sharp end, the cowboy cuts a circle around the horn and digs it out, leaving a small circular wound that heals quickly. Larger horns are removed with a dehorner, a mechanical clipper, or with a dehorning saw. It is possible to dehorn animals with electric horn irons, but I have never seen this method used and don't know anything about it.

One inevitable result of dehorning is loss of blood. A small calf dehorned with a tube may bleed very little, while a large animal that is dehorned with a saw may spurt blood for a long time—an hour, two hours, or half a day. Some ranchers simply let nature take care of this problem, but others argue that the bleeding weakens the calf and that it should be controlled.

I have seen three methods used to control horn bleeding. The first involves the application of a powder called blood-stopper. Whether it does the cattle any good, I don't know, but I do know that, on a windy day, it ends up in the eyes and mouths of the cowboys. A second method is cauterizing with a hot iron, either a branding iron or a specially built horn iron. The wound is seared until the major vessels have been sealed and the bleeding has either stopped or slowed to a trickle. The third method is called "pulling the veins," which is the approach used by veterinarians when they have to dehorn an animal. Using a pair of surgical clamps (hemostats), you locate the major veins that have been severed. The ones that bleed the most lie between the base of the horn and the ear. You clamp them with the hemostats and pull them so that they break off beneath the skin. This technique is slow and tedious, it requires some knowledge of bovine anatomy, and it is difficult to perform unless the animal is confined in a chute.

Every ranch will have its own approach to working cattle on branding day, and its own methods of castrating and dehorning. Ranch folks rarely argue the pros and cons of these methods or try to convince their neighbors that they are going about it the wrong way. One man will swear by one philosophy and his neighbor will swear by another. On sale day, when both bunches run through the livestock auction, a third party would swear that there isn't a nickle's worth of difference between them.

12

Summer Work

A more pleasant summer job on the ranch is riding pastures.

On a cow-calf ranch, the first job of the summer begins after the spring branding when the calves are turned out. Freshly worked calves go through a period of stress which may last only a few days or up to a week. Stress is caused by several factors: loss of blood, the shock of dehorning and castration, soreness, and even a reaction to the vaccine. In small calves the stress is usually not severe. Their horns are small and the surgery that removes them is not radical, and the same holds true of their castration, so they don't lose much blood and don't suffer much shock. For several days they may lie around, their heads will be sore, and they may not drink much milk. But after that they bounce right back and are healed up in a week's time. The healing process takes longer with larger calves, and they are the ones most vulnerable to stress. One day a nice, fat steer calf is walking slowly or lying off to himself, which you expect to see in a large calf that is stiff and sore. Then the next day you find him dead. You can never be sure exactly what it was that killed him, but you assume it had something to do with stress.

Another problem you check for in freshly worked cattle is "bugs"—screwworms or maggots in the horn cavities and scrotums. Screwworms and maggots are both fly larvae, and the untrained observer cannot distinguish one from the other. But there is an enormous difference between the two,

148

for while the maggot lives on dead flesh, the screwworm attacks living flesh and can actually eat an animal to death. Screwworms used to be the scourge of the cattle business, and cowboys spent much of their time in the early summer roping and doctoring cattle for screwworms. In a bad screwworm year, death losses could be staggering. I am old enough to have doctored for screwworms in the late 1950s, but most young cowboys today have never had the pleasure of pouring medicine into the horn cavity of a calf and stirring out a cupful of bugs. It was foul business. Young cowboys have missed out on this because the governments of the United States and Mexico launched a screwworm eradication program that has enjoyed remarkable success. Nowadays, in a typical year, a hundred or so screwworm cases will be reported in South Texas and the southern states, but in the Texas and Oklahoma panhandles, and points further north, the screwworm has been virtually extinct since the 1960s.

What you find now in freshly worked calves is maggots—or at least that is what you assume they are, maggots instead of a freak case of screwworms. Some ranchers don't bother to doctor for maggots, reasoning that the maggots eat only dead tissue out of a wound and then drop off. Other ranchers take the opposite view, arguing that even though maggots are theoretically benign, they have no business working inside a calf's head and they are up to no good.

A case of bugs is easy to spot if you are familiar with the signs. When they are present in the scrotum, the bag will be swollen and you can see a brownish discharge on the inside of the animal's legs. The same brownish fluid can be seen around a horn wound that is hosting maggots. Also, a calf with maggots in its horn cavity will tend to shake its head or hold it at a peculiar angle. In either location, maggots can be detected easily by any cowboy who has ever doctored them before. They produce a foul odor that you can smell twenty or thirty feet away, and once you've smelled it you'll never forget it.

A week after the spring roundup, all the calves should be healed up and over the stress period, and the cowboy can go on to the other summer jobs. If he uses his head, he will try to get his fencing work done as early in the season as possible. In the panhandle regions of Texas and Oklahoma, spring rains usually fall from mid-April to mid-June, and after that the weather turns hot and we get blast-furnace winds from the southwest. The hot winds sap moisture from the ground, and as any cowboy who has worked on the blister-end of a posthole digger knows, it is easier to dig a hole when the soil is damp. By August the ground is often baked so hard that, in order to dig a posthole, you may have to chip the ground with a sharpened bar, dig it out to a depth of six or eight inches, fill the hole with water, let it stand and soak, dig down another foot, fill it up again and let it stand, until you reach the depth of two and a half or three feet.

The kind of fence we're talking about here is barbed wire fence, which will consist of three, four, or five strands of wire stapled to posts that are set anywhere from ten to twenty feet apart. A cowboy may be in charge of maintaining thirty or forty miles of this fence, and it is a job that never ends. A fence built within the last ten years, which has solid posts and good galvanized wire, will require little maintainance and care. The cowboy can load up a boot top of staples and a hammer, climb on his horse, and start riding fence, tacking it up where the staples have popped out.

But then there's the other kind of fence that is much more common. This kind was built thirty or forty years ago. The wire is rusted and brittle, and the posts may be so rotten that they will no longer hold a staple. Some ranches pursue an agressive maintainance program and replace large numbers of posts every spring. The cowboys are told that if they can push on an old post and break it off, it should be replaced. But it would be safe to say that most ranches don't operate this way. There never seems to be enough time to fix the fences the way they should be fixed, and as long as a fence is standing, as long as the wires are tacked to the posts, and as long as it turns cattle, it is regarded as a good fence. As the price of posts and wire continues to rise, this philosophy becomes more respectable, and the fence is patched and cobbled until it begins to leak cattle, at which time drastic action is demanded. This might mean planting a few new posts and stretching up a few strands of new wire, or it might mean that the entire fence line has to be torn out and replaced. But fencing material has become so expensive that this step is avoided for as long as possible.

I believe it was Robert Frost who said that good fences make good neighbors. That is a wise saying, and ranch folks who have never heard of Robert Frost quote it all the time. One of the least-loved characters in the West is the rancher who won't keep up his fences, especially if his cattle stray over into the neighbor's pasture. It is an unwritten law in ranch country that he whose cattle stray has an obligation to fix the fence until they strayeth not. If he doesn't, he is not considered a very good neighbor, and his popularity begins to wane.

Most ranchers have a sensible attitude toward stray cattle. They understand that, under certain conditions, anyone's cattle will stray. Today it's yours, tomorrow it will be mine. And as long as the owner of the stray cattle demonstrates a responsible attitude, tries to keep his cattle in, and does some work on the fences, no one is offended. However, if the owner of the strays doesn't show a responsible attitude, he is likely to encounter hostility. After a man has put his neighbor's cattle out three or four times, after he has called the man and told him that something must be done, his temper rises and he begins to think of nasty things to do. And they can be very nasty.

The offended rancher may tell his cowboys that if they want to practice roping and busting cattle, they can go to work on the neighbor's stock. He may load the strays in a trailer, haul them five miles away, and turn them out in the middle of a county road. Or he may haul them to the nearest livestock auction and leave them in a pen, telling the county sheriff that he found some strays and that the sheriff can trace the brand and contact the owner. By the time the owner is notified, his cattle have run up a feed bill at the sale barn, and this not-so-subtle hint tells him that his neighbor is unhappy, and that maybe it's time to leave the coffee shop and go plant a few fence posts.

I once knew a rancher whose neighbor's bulls simply would not stay at home. He put them out one day and the next they were right back again. He called the neighbor and talked to him. He pleaded. He raged. Nothing happened, and he turned to dirty tricks. The next time he saw the stray bulls in his pasture, he ordered the hired man to drive the pickup and chase the bulls, and at thirty miles an hour, the rancher leaned out the right-hand window, firing a twelve-gauge shotgun loaded with birdshot.

I heard the story of another rancher who was so sick and tired of putting out his neighbor's bull that he went to town and bought himself a bull whip. He went out a-horseback and drove the bull five miles at a run, whipping him all the way. He drove the bull right into his neighbor's front yard, where the beast collapsed and died. That's what you call sendin' the folks a message.

There are four parts to a fence: corners, gates, water gaps, and the straight-line fence. Building fence is a craft that requires knowledge and skill, and the cowboy must be competent in fence engineering. All the wires are

A braced corner in a four-wire barbed wire fence.

stretched tight with a device called a "come-along," or wire stretcher. Since a line of fence will produce considerable tension, the corners must be braced and reinforced, otherwise the corner post will be pulled over. A properly constructed fence corner will consist of a heavy corner post and two brace posts sitting at right angles, connected by a piece of pipe or lumber and pulled together with several strands of twisted wire that run from the bottom of the corner to the top of the brace post. The fence must also be braced on both sides of a gate, or at any other point where the wire is stretched. Hence, a normal fence line will follow this pattern: braced corner, line fence, braced terminal post, gate, braced terminal post, line fence, and braced corner.

Gates may be constructed of wood or welded pipe, but the most common gate is one made of four to six barbed wires tied to gate sticks and connected at both ends to braced terminal posts. One of the gate sticks is connected to the terminal post by wire loops and can be opened and thrown back to allow traffic to pass. County roads or oil-field roads that pass through open range employ a device known as the cattleguard, or as some old-timers call it, a "corrugate." The cattleguard consists of a rectangular frame of heavy pipe, crossed horizontally by smaller pipes spaced at four- or five-inch intervals. The ground beneath it has been dug out, and the principle of the cattleguard is that cattle and horses will not walk across it. Usually it works, but from time to time the pit fills up with dirt and the stock begin walking across it. When that occurs, the county usually gets an angry phone call from the rancher, and a few days later a crew comes out, moves the cattleguard, and digs out the pit.

A water gap (sometimes called a floodgate) solves the problem of how to build a fence across a creek, river, or ravine that carries a large amount of water after a rain. If you did not put a water gap into such places, if you just

A water gap, or flood gate, across the Beaver River.

Fencing equipment, clockwise from upper left: wire stretchers, or come-alongs, posthole diggers, tamping bar, baling wire, a boot top of staples, staples, and wire pliers.

built a regular fence across a river, the first time the river came up, driftwood and weeds would collect on the wires, and when the pressure became great enough, posts would break off, staples would pop, wires would break, and the entire fence line would be taken out and destroyed. After you had rebuilt half a mile of fence, you would put in a water gap.

A water gap is just a gate or token fence that crosses a watercourse. It is usually made of old wire and old posts, and you build it knowing that when the water comes up, the gap will wash out. You want it to wash out so that the pressure of flood water does not destroy the rest of the fence. Ranchers along the Beaver River in the Oklahoma Panhandle can expect their water gaps to go out every time the river comes up, which may be four or five times a year. When the water level recedes, the cowboys put on shorts and tennis shoes, load up some old wire and old posts, and spend a day or two rebuilding the water gaps.

In his fencing work, the cowboy uses several pieces of special equipment: posthole diggers, a tamping bar to pack the soil around a post, wire stretchers, fence staples, and wire pliers. Wire pliers are designed specifically for fence work, and with them the cowboy can pull an old staple out of a post, cut heavy wire, drive a staple, and if he knows how to use them, he can even do a limited amount of stretching with them. Many cowboys carry a pair of wire pliers on their saddles, so that when they're out a-horseback they can fix broken fence or "build a gate" in a fence line when they need to go after an ornery cow brute.

There are four kinds of fence posts used these days: bodark (properly spelled in the French *bois d'arc,* and often called "hedge" or "hedge apple"), cedar, creosote-treated pine, and steel. A good bodark post is hard to beat, and it will last for forty or fifty years. The major disadvantage of bodark is that, once it has cured out, it becomes so hard that you can hardly drive a staple into it. A good red-cedar post with a seven- or eight-inch butt also makes excellent fencing material, but good cedar is getting hard to find. Much of the cedar sold today is a fast-growing variety that will rot out to the heart in ten years or less. Creosote-treated pine posts are most commonly used in corral fences, probably because they are too expensive to be used in line fences that run for miles. Steel posts are seeing more and more use these days, and their primary advantage is that they require very little maintainance, since the barbed wire is affixed to the post with galvanized fence stay instead of staples. However, steel posts are not as substantial as the wooden varieties, and they are easily bent by scratching cows and fighting bulls.

A more pleasant summer job on the ranch is riding pastures. "Prowling" is the old-time word for this job, and it is highly descriptive of what the cowboy does. You could say that he "rides" the pasture, but that would not capture the essential nature of the work. When he rides pastures in the summertime, he is prowling around and looking for problems. It isn't necessary to prowl pastures in the winter, or at least it's optional, because the cowboy has the opportunity to look over the cattle every day on the feed ground.

On some outfits the prowling is done in a pickup. In the heat of the day, when most of the cattle are gathered around windmills and waterholes, someone drives through the pasture, hits the waterholes, and looks the cattle over. This method is easier on the humans, but it doesn't always work in pastures that are big or rough.

When the cowboy prowls a-horseback, he studies the grass and the range conditions to determine if the pasture is being overgrazed. He checks the windmills and waterholes to be sure the cattle have an adequate supply of

Roping and doctoring pinkeye in the pasture, one of the routine summer jobs on a ranch. Here, Erickson and Calipso move in on a black baldface yearling steer that is blind in his right eye.

Erickson ropes the steer by the neck, and Tom Ellzey and Happy move in for a heel shot.

With the steer stretched out on the ground, Ellzey and Erickson go to work on his eye. They have thrown a half-hitch over their dallies to hold the ropes to the horns while their horses hold the steer down.

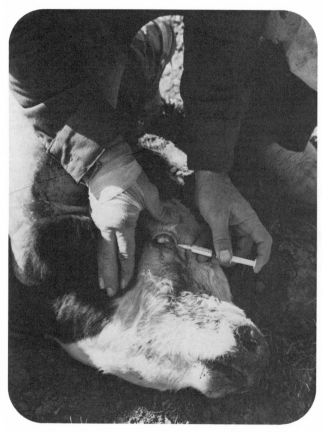

Here Ellzey takes from his medicine bag that he carries on his belt a small syringe which he fills with medicine. Slipping the small-gauge needle under the outer layer of tissue on the eyeball, he injects two cc's, causing a small, white bubble to form beneath the tissue.

Finally Ellzey glues a patch of cloth over the steer's eye, which shuts out dust and sunlight. In two or three weeks, the patch will fall off, and usually by then the eye has healed.

clean water. He checks the salt licks. He observes any unusual patterns in the movement of wildlife. If he sees a buzzard in the sky or a coyote moving around in the daylight, it might mean nothing, or it might mean that scavengers are feeding on a dead animal. If this is the case, the cowboy wants to find the carcass and determine the cause of death.

When he comes to cattle in a bunch, he will look them over, checking brands, eyes, udders, everything. He will study the cows for signs of lump-jaw and cancer-eye. He will check the calves for pinkeye, and if he is carrying medicine, he may rope and doctor them on the spot. If the pasture is small enough, he may try to get a count on the cattle, writing the tally down on the palm of his hand or on a matchbook cover. In big pastures and in herds of more than seventy or eighty cattle, counting can be very difficult.

In our part of the country, summer work on a cow-calf outfit doesn't include much handling or moving of cattle. After the spring roundup when the cattle are located in their summer pastures, they often are not rounded up again until fall unless there is a special reason for it. This is not the case in other parts of the country, especially in humid regions where ticks, flies, and other parasites are a constant problem. There, cattle must be gathered periodically and sprayed.

If the ranch feeds hay during the winter months, that hay will have to be laid in during the summer. Some ranches purchase all their hay from the outside and have it hauled in by the semi-truck load. If the ranch has some good bottom land or an open meadow, this country might be emptied of cattle in the spring and the grass allowed to grow. Then, in July or August, the grass will be mowed and baled up into prairie hay, which makes good winter feed for cattle and is excellent horse feed. Or the ranch might have a patch of irrigated alfalfa, in which case the cowboy crew will spend a large part of the summer watering, mowing, raking, baling, and hauling hay.

But the most important summer job of all, at least in this semiarid country, involves water. Cattle can live with pinkeye and short grass and shabby fences, but they can survive only a few hot days without water. Maintaining windmills is such a crucial part of the cowboy's summer routine that I will devote the next chapter to it.

13
Windmills

The windmill is a simple machine that performs the simple function of raising a small amount of water from the ground. It consists of three parts: the tower, the head, and the hole.

The most conspicuous part of the windmill, and the one most people associate with the name, is the tower. That is the structure you see in the distance when you are driving through the prairie states. There are no moving parts in the tower, no machinery. It's just a scaffold, usually with four legs, that holds the head and fan above the ground where they can be exposed to a constant flow of wind. It may be as short as fifteen feet or as tall as fifty. In the early days all towers were made of wood, and a few of them have survived to the present day. Most are a horror to climb because the wood is rotten and you can never be sure when the piece you're standing on is going to turn into daylight. Most of the old wooden towers have been replaced by structures made of galvanized angle iron or welded pipe. The legs are either set in cement or bolted to posts set deep into the ground. This gives the tower a firm foundation that will keep it standing upright even in a high wind.

The device that is perched on top of the tower is the motor, which converts wind into mechanical energy, and it can be divided into three components: the fan, the head, and the tail. The fan of a modern windmill is con-

It has been the only piece of machinery the cowboy has ever fully understood.

163

structed of galvanized steel blades that are curved to catch the wind and are connected to a hub by steel spokes. The diameter of the fan determines the amount of energy it produces and the amount of water it can pump. A six-foot fan can service a shallow well of, say, twenty to sixty feet. A deeper well, one going down to two hundred feet, will require an eight-foot fan. And very deep wells, those going down to four hundred feet or more, will require a fan of ten or twelve feet. When you buy a new fan, it comes in sections which can be hoisted to the top of the tower by a rope and bolted together. If part of the fan thrashes in a high wind, the defective section can be replaced with a new one, and the job can be done on the tower by one man with a wrench and a set of vice-grip pliers.

The tail serves several functions. It provides a counterbalance to the weight of the fan. It holds the fan into the wind, turning the head on its pivot so that it adjusts automatically to changes in the direction of the wind. And it also serves as an automatic shutoff in a dangerously high wind. The tail is spring-loaded, so that when the wind reaches a certain velocity, it folds back against the fan and activates the braking system, either slowing the fan down or shutting it off entirely.

The third windmill component that sits on top of the tower contains the guts of the mill. It is called the head or motor, and it sits between the fan and the tail. The fan is connected to a horizontal shaft which runs into the cast-iron housing of the head. The shaft moves on roller bearings and turns with the fan. Through a system of gears inside the head, the whirling of the fan is translated into an up-and-down motion, called the stroke. It is this stroke that brings the water to the surface.

The windmill motor is a simple mechanical device composed of shafts, bearings, and gears, which means that even cowboys, who are not famous for their comprehension of machinery, can figure out how it works, what is wrong with it, and how it can be repaired. A man armed with nothing but a pair of pliers can gut completely an Aermotor head in twenty minutes. The Dempster head is a bit more complicated, but still within the range of the average cowboy's ability.

The third part of the windmill begins below the head, and it consists of jet rod (or sucker rod), checks, pipe, casing, and a working barrel. Jet rod is most often made of wood, and it comes in lengths ranging from ten to twenty-five feet. Each section has two metal ends, one with male threads and the other with female threads. The rods are screwed together and lowered into the pipe, which runs from the top of the ground into the sand formation containing the water. The pipe is usually two-inch galvanized, though the diameter of the pipe can vary. It sits inside the casing, usually made of eight-inch plastic or steel. The casing lines the hole and prevents cave-ins, and it cannot be removed. The two-inch pipe can be taken out.

So we have eight-inch casing and two-inch pipe. Both run from the ground down to the water in the well. The jet rods run from the head at the top of the tower into the two-inch pipe and down to the bottom of the hole, where the pumping mechanism is located. The pump consists of a brass tube, called a working barrel or cylinder, which screws onto the last joint of two-inch pipe. Sitting inside the bottom of the cylinder is the bottom check, which, by means of a simple ball valve, allows water to enter the cylinder. The water is taken up by the top check, which is connected to the last joint of jet rod. The jet rod is fastened to the head at the top of the tower, and the up-and-down stroke in the machinery raises the jet rod up and down. Every time the mill goes through a cycle, the jet rod and the top check move one stroke in the cylinder. The top check is equipped with the same kind of ball valve as the bottom check, except that when the bottom check lets water into the cylinder and holds it, the top check moves it up the pipe and holds it. The watertight seal on both checks is provided by the leathers, cups of leather which fit around the checks and which, when saturated with water, expand against the cylinder walls to make a seal. If the leathers are worn or defective, the suction in the cylinder is lost and the mill will not pump.

This all sounds dreadfully complicated, which only goes to prove that the simplest functions are sometimes the most difficult to explain in writing. But there is nothing complicated about a windmill, and that's the beauty of it. The reader who has choked on all this business of heads and tails, rods and pipes, cylinders and checks, will just have to take my word for it: windmills are simple. If they weren't, I wouldn't be writing about them.

Maintaining windmills and keeping them running is an important part of the modern cowboy's job, and most cowboys know enough about windmill technology to diagnose and repair most problems that develop. In caring for windmills, you run into a lot of small problems and only a few big ones. The small ones can be fixed by one man. If the head is squeaking, it probably needs oil. Standard windmill oil is thin; twenty-weight oil is recommended by the manufacturers. But I have known cowboys who thought that heavier oil was better, and I even knew one man in Beaver County who used nothing but straight STP oil treatment, which is as thick as honey. If a fan section has thrashed, you replace it with a new one. If the jet rod that runs from the tower down to the ground has broken off in the wind, you stick a new one in.

There are other problems which can be corrected by one man, but which are much easier with two. If the mill stops pumping water, you assume (1) the leathers on the top check are worn, (2) the top check itself is worn, or (3) the ball in the top check is not seating properly, in which case the check can be dressed with a file and put back into the hole. To get the top check out of the hole, you must pull the rods. In a shallow well, you may have only twenty feet of rods. In a deep well, you may have two hundred, three hundred, or four hundred feet. The rods are soaked up with water, and they are heavy. Two men can pull the rods out of a two-hundred-foot well and work up a good sweat. If the well is much deeper than that, it may require the use of a block and tackle or a pickup with a front-end winch.

If the top check seems to be in good shape, if the leathers are not worn out, then the problem may lie in the bottom check. Windmilling turns into work when you have to go back for the bottom check. After pulling all the rods out to get the top check, you must screw them all back together, go back into the hole, and fish for the bottom check. This is a job you want to give to your most experienced windmill man, because when you're standing 150 feet away from the two pieces of metal you're trying to join, it isn't easy to determine when you've got a good bite. Sometimes you pull out the rods only to learn that you didn't get the bottom check. You're tired and hot and your arms ache, but you have to go back into the hole and fish again. Sometimes you snag the bottom check by one thread, and just as you get it to the top of the hole, it comes loose and falls back to the bottom. That is very depressing on a hot July afternoon.

Bottom checks do not wear as quickly as top checks, because a bottom check sits inside the cylinder and does not move. Occasionally you will find one with a worn seat or ball, but the most common problem I have encountered with bottom checks is an accumulation of mud and jet-rod shavings which keeps the ball valve from seating properly.

If there is nothing wrong with the bottom check, and if the windmill still won't pump when you've put it all back together, then you have to pull the pipe, which is a big job. Unless the well is very shallow, you will need some special equipment: two snatch blocks, pipe dogs, about seventy feet of cable, two twenty-four-inch pipe wrenches, and a pickup with enough power to raise a long string of pipe—or, better yet, one equipped with an electric winch. Two men can pull pipe, but the job goes more smoothly with three: one to operate the winch, one to watch the pipe dog over the hole, and the third to stack the pipe up in the tower. When you pull pipe out of a well, you are looking for two kinds of problems: holes in the pipe that might allow water to run back into the well, and holes in the working barrel that would cause the checks to lose their suction. In either case, you replace the worn part. If that was your problem, then you're back in the water business.

But if, after you've pulled the pipe and checked the cylinder, you still don't get water, then the chances are that you have lost the well, in which case you have to call a water-well-drilling contractor and have him dig you another one.

When I managed a ranch in Beaver County, Oklahoma, I did most of the maintenance work on nine windmills, swapping out help with the neighbors for the bigger jobs like pulling pipe. But there were times when I needed to take down the head, and since I didn't have the equipment for that, I called the windmill man. There were three or four of them within a radius of sixty miles, and usually I could get one of them to come out within a day or two. They had trucks that were specially designed for windmill work. With a hydraulic boom and power take-off winch, they could pull the head off a windmill and have it on the ground in half an hour or less. They also carried a stock of parts with them, so that they could take care of most problems without running back to town.

Some ranchers choose not to bother with windmill work at all. I knew of one ranch on the Beaver River that had about thirty windmills, and the cowboys on this outfit never touched a jet-rod wrench or a snatch block. The manager had a service contract with a local windmill man who took care of everything from major repairs to oiling the mills twice a year. But this type of arrangement is not very common. A few giant ranches, such as the 6666 Ranch at Guthrie, Texas, have so many windmills that they keep a full-time windmill man on the payroll.

Windmills have been at work in the American West for a hundred years, and during that time they have been improved and refined, but the basic design and concept have changed very little. Every now and then a shade-tree inventor will come up with a modified design (chain-drive instead of gear-drive, a slightly different style of fan or tail), but these new versions have not caught on, and the windmill market remains firmly in the hands of two companies, Aermotor and Dempster. The fact that windmills have changed so little during this century of rapid technological advance indicates that the basic windmill design was sound to start with and has remained that way over the years. Yet I have a feeling that thinking on the subject has atrophied, and that the day is coming when engineers and inventors will take a fresh look at the old ranch windmill and start experimenting with new concepts and new ways of harnessing the wind. The impetus for this will come from two economic forces: the rising cost of windmill parts and the rising cost of all forms of energy.

Both forces are already at work. In the past five years, windmill parts (fan sections, tails, heads, shafts, bearings) have become terribly expensive, even though Dempster and Aermotor have both begun manufacturing their parts abroad to avoid the high cost of American labor. Jet rods are very ex-

Working on top of a windmill tower. Picture shows platform, tail, head, and fan.

Pulling pipe out of a broken windmill with a block and tackle is a three-man job.

pensive, and so is steel pipe. And all of a sudden, ranchers are taking a cold, hard look at their windmills and wondering if they can afford to keep them. The economic equation has changed to such a degree that, even with free energy (wind), the windmill has become a marginal piece of machinery that requires too much expensive steel and too many expensive parts.

Many ranchers are junking out their windmills and installing electric submersible pumps. One version of this approach employs one large, centrally located pump that is connected to outlying tanks through a network of plastic pipe. The electric pump offers several advantages over the windmill. It doesn't require a tower, it doesn't use jet rods, it has fewer moving parts, it produces a much larger volume of water, and, most important of all, you can buy an electric motor and pump for about what you would pay for a new windmill head and fan. On the negative side, electric pumps are complicated and temperamental, and maintaining them can be a pain in the neck. But the most damning argument against electric pumps is that they are hooked into the conventional power system (no hedge against brownouts or power failures), and they are inescapably linked to a source of energy that is becoming more expensive every year.

At the moment, the bottom line says that windmills have had their day and are on the way out, and that stock water can be pumped more economically with electric motors. But I suspect that there is a bottomer line which says "Clever people that we are, we had better come up with a better, more efficient windmill design and take full advantage of all that free wind that blows across the prairie." If pipes and towers and fans and jet rods and replacement parts have become too expensive, then we will design a windmill that doesn't need those things. Let's junk the old concept, which, after all, was born a hundred years ago in the era of cheap steel and cheap labor, and

This experimental windcharger was built in Clayton, New Mexico, by NASA and the Department of Energy. The wind turbine consists of two sixty-three-foot propeller blades and thirty tons of machinery, sitting on the top of a one hundred-foot tower. A computer automatically reads shifts in wind direction and aligns the blades. The turbine generates up to two hundred kilowats of electricity and reduces the town's dependence on diesel-powered generators.

build a windmill that meets the needs of modern ranch economics. We can throw out everything except the most basic and most important part of the windmill—*wind,* which is still free, abundant, and untaxable.

Someone in the windmill business has already started thinking in this direction. In 1978 I was driving through the Oklahoma Panhandle and saw a strange device sitting out on the baldies. It looked like a toy windmill. A very small fan sat on top of a tower that couldn't have been more than eight or ten feet high. I made inquiries about this and was told that it was a new kind of windmill. Instead of using the old-fashioned, strictly mechanical approach to pumping water, this machine used wind power to produce air pressure, which forced water out of the ground and to the surface. I don't know the name of the company who produced this machine, and I don't know how well it has performed out in the pasture. But whoever made that windmill was thinking in the right direction. Here is a radically different concept in wind technology. This mill is smaller and therefore less expensive than the old-style mill. It has fewer moving parts, it doesn't require a working barrel, checks, jet rods, or two-inch pipe. All the working parts are on the surface where they can be easily maintained, and it is small enough to be moved from place to place in the back of a pickup.

That's a good start, but there may be even better designs awaiting our inventors. What about hydraulics? What about wind-generated electricity, or a combination of wind-generated electricity and solar power? What about a vertical-axis turbine, similar to the one the USDA has built at the Bushland, Texas, experiment station?

These are just ideas, and we are still years away from an economical, well-engineered alternative to the old-style windmill. In the meantime, more and more ranchers will replace their windmills with submersible pumps, and the day may come when the friendly old windmill will disappear from the prairie country. It won't be the same without the windmill turning in the breeze, and the old cowboy will mourn its passing. For many years it has been a friend and a provider of fresh water. But more important, it has been the only piece of machinery the cowboy has ever fully understood.

14

The Fall Work

The fall work comes at a time of year when the weather in prairie country becomes a major concern.

When the cow-calf rancher goes into the fall roundup season, he will have four goals in mind: brand and work the summer calves, sort the cattle and move them to winter pastures, cull the herd, and ship the calves. Of the four, the last is the most important.

Shipping day is the most important day of the year on any cow-calf ranch. For the rancher, it is payday. Though he may sell off a few cull cows during the year and may elect to sell a small bunch of calves in the spring, most of his income from cattle is generated in the fall of the year. After shipping day, he will sit down with a calculator, run all the figures on weight, gain, and price per pound, and decide whether his year's work brought him a profit or a loss.

On the typical cow-calf ranch in our part of the world, most of the calves hit the ground between January and April. These calves are branded and worked at spring roundup. On summer range they receive nourishment from their mothers' milk and also begin eating grass as they get older. They grow and gain weight, and by October they should weigh between 375 and 550 pounds. Calves on the lighter end will included the youngest, calves of first-calf heifers, and calves that are runty because their mothers do not produce enough milk. Calves on the heavier end will be the oldest and those

174

whose mothers are good milk producers. A good average pay weight on a set of calves in the Panhandle would be around 450 pounds. Calf weights will be higher in a good grass year and lower in a bad year, higher in crossbred calves and lower in straightbreds. These "four-weight" calves are the basic cash crop of a cow-calf operation. Calves of this weight are bought from the ranch by stocker, or yearling, operators who will graze them through the winter months on wheat pasture, oat pasture, or stalk fields, and take them up to feeder weight, around 600 or 700 pounds.

In the fall of the year, the rancher studies the cattle market and his range conditions, sets his shipping date, and assembles a cowboy crew. Let's say that he is going to sell his calves through a livestock auction, which means that he will contact the auction manager a week or two in advance and consign the calves for a certain day. Then he must line up cattle trucks and make arrangements for hauling the calves to the sale barn.

On roundup morning, the cowboy crew assembles at daylight and begins rounding up the first pasture. When the cattle are pushed into the shipping pens, the cowboys dismount and begin cutting out the cows and bulls, leaving the calves in the pen. When this is done, they mount up and ride to the next pasture, gather the herd, pen them, and sort off the cows and bulls. This procedure may be repeated three or four times, depending on the number of pastures the rancher intends to ship.

At a shipping roundup, there is little time for foolishness or play. The work must be done quickly because the roundup is only one part of a chain of events. At ten o'clock the trucks will arrive and be ready to load cattle. When the calves are loaded and trucked to the livestock auction, they will have to be sized and sexed (sorted into smaller bunches according to weight, sex, and sometimes appearance and breed), and at two o'clock they are sched-

In the fall of the year, the days turn crisp and a cowboy digs out his warm clothes: shotgun chaps, flannel shirt, down-filled vest, felt hat, and bandanna.

uled to be sold. The crew operates under a time deadline, and they are aware that the minute the cattle enter a corral, they begin losing weight—shrinking. Back in the old days, most cattle were sold by the head and nobody worried about shrink. Today, they are sold by the pound, and shrink is a major concern because weight lost is money lost.

There is another method the rancher might use at shipping time. Instead of selling his calf crop through a sale ring, he can sell them right from the ranch. On bigger ranches, this is the preferred method of doing business. The rancher gets in touch with the cattle buyers, makes his own deal, and weighs the calves on scales at the ranch. The owner of a small ranch has the option of selling this way, but he may not have a good set of scales or enough calves to interest an outside buyer, and he may find it more convenient to deal through a livestock auction.

When the cattle are sold directly from the ranch, the roundup might begin several days before the shipping date, when the cowboy crew goes from one end of the ranch to the other, gathering the cattle in all the summer pastures. In each pasture the herd is driven to a corner of a fence, and while the cowboys hold herd, the boss rides in and begins sexing the cattle, separating the steer and heifer calves and pairing them up with their mothers. The calves must be sexed because steers bring more money than heifers, and therefore they must be weighed in separate bunches. We'll say that on the first cut, the rancher sorts off cows with heifer calves. These are held outside the main herd by two or three cowboys until the sorting is done. When the herd has been split, the crew is divided up, and one crew drives the heifer herd to one holding pasture, or "trap," while the second crew drives the steer herd to another. The traps are small pastures located near the shipping pens, and they are stocked only during the few days before shipping day, which means that they have enough grass to sustain a large herd of animals for a short period of time.

On shipping day, you have all your steers in one trap and all the heifers in another. Both are near the shipping pens. You don't have to gather the whole ranch, you don't have to drive the cattle a long distance, and you don't have to waste time separating steers and heifers. This approach is more than a convenience; it is a shrewd business practice. The rancher knows that the longer it takes him to gather, sort, and weigh the calves, the more weight they will lose to shrink. Through careful planning, he has figured out a way of cutting his shrink to a bare minimum.

As soon as the cattle are driven into the pens and the gate is shut behind them, the cowboys tie their horses and begin sorting off the cows and bulls, and immediately the calves are driven into the scale pen in bunches of fifteen or twenty. As soon as they are weighed, they are loaded into the waiting trucks. When the trucks pull away from the corrals, the rancher and the buyer are still in the scale house, adding up the weights, figuring the "pencil shrink," and coming up with the pay weight.

Shipping the calf crop is the focal point of the fall roundup season, but other jobs must be attended to as well. After the calves are shipped, their mothers, now dry cows, will be gathered and driven to winter pastures where they will remain until spring. Ideally, a winter pasture is located in low country, perhaps on a river bottom, where the cattle will have some natural protection from winter storms, and close to headquarters so that the cowboys can always get feed to them, even in bad weather.

While the rancher has his dry cows assembled, he will take the opportunity to cull his herd, which is a very important part of ranch management. He cuts out old cows, thin cows, cripples, bad-eyes, lump-jaws, and any

This shot shows how we use a squeeze chute for the job of dehorning yearling cattle. On a yearling operation, this is one of the fall jobs that must be done before the steers are taken to wheat pasture for the winter. Tom Ellzey is using a big clipper-type dehorner that can cut off big horns at the base of the head. I am standing by with a hot searing iron which Tom will use to cauterize the head wounds and stop the bleeding.

other cows he doesn't want to carry through the winter. Fall is the best time to cull the herd, since the calves have been pulled off and shipped and the problem of pairing up cows and calves is thus avoided. When all the culls are sorted off and thrown together, they will be hauled to a livestock auction and sold as packer cows. If the rancher does not cull his herd in the fall, if he doesn't cull deeply enough, and if he leaves old, thin stock in the herd, they might not make it through the winter, and he will lose their salvage value.

Finally, if the rancher has some summer calves (calves that have been born since the spring branding), he will get them worked and branded while he has his cowboy crew assembled. As a rule, fall brandings are not large and are not the festive occasions that spring brandings are, but this is work that has to be done.

The fall work comes at a time of year when the weather in prairie country becomes a major concern. The rancher wants to hold his calf crop as long as he can because he is selling by the pound and wants his calves to gain every pound possible. But after the first frost, the grass begins to lose its strength. Both cows and calves stop gaining weight, and they may even start going backward. If the rancher waits too long to sell, holding out for more gain or a better market, he may wake up one morning and find snow on the ground. At the very best, this means that the cattle will lose weight in the bad weather. At the worst, it could mean that the roads into the ranch would now be impassable for trucks, in which case he might not be able to sell his calves. He will have to wean them and carry them through the winter, which in turn means more work, more risk, and higher feed bills. If he holds the calves over until spring and the market drops, he can suffer a considerable financial loss.

When the fall work is all done, when the calves are shipped, the culls sent to town, the dry cows settled on winter pastures, and the summer calves worked and branded, then the cowboy puts his horses out to pasture, hangs up his spurs, and begins his winter feed run. The cycle has begun again. For the next four months he will fight mud and snow, biting winds, and boredom. And he will look forward to that day in April when he fills his lungs with sweet air, catches that first whiff of green grass, and knows that spring roundup is a-coming.

15
Calving Out Heifers

A heifer is a young female, a young cow. Many ranchers routinely save back a certain percentage of each year's heifers, grow them to breeding age, calve them out, and then work them into the herd to replace brood cows that have been culled. This is a long and expensive process. When a heifer is held back for breeding purposes, she is at least two and sometimes three years away from her first calf, and until she gets that first calf on the ground—indeed, until that first calf is sold—a heifer merely eats and takes up space. She makes the ranch no money whatever. For this reason, some ranchers take the position that saving heifers is a losing proposition, and instead of raising their own replacement animals, they prefer to buy young cows on the market. The rule of thumb I have heard is that any time you can sell two heifers and buy one cow for the same money, you should do it.

In the fall of year one, the rancher looks over his heifers and cuts out the ones he wants to save as replacements. We'll say he cuts out fifty. In selecting replacement heifers, he wants the very best. If he does his cutting in a pen on shipping day, when all the heifer calves are together, he may walk through the bunch and make his choices on the strength of appearance. If the heifer looks good as a calf, the chances are that she will look good as a cow. *Good* might mean several things: the way she walks, her coloring and

"I've been calving out heifers all my life, and every year I know less about them than I did before."

181

This bunch of Hereford heifers has just been taken off their mommas and turned into a weaning pen. In about two years, they will deliver their first calves, and the cowboy in charge will have to nurse them through the experience.

markings, her overall conformation, the appearance of her head, her size, and so forth. Or the rancher's choice might be guided by a completely different philosophy. I knew a rancher who used to cut all his replacement heifers out of a herd while the cows and calves were paired up. He didn't even look at the calf; he looked at the calf's *mother,* reasoning that a good cow will produce a good heifer calf, and that he could more accurately predict what a heifer would look like three years in the future by observing her mother than by observing the calf herself.

Through one method or another, we assemble a set of fifty heifers in year one, when they are approximately six months old and weigh about four hundred pounds. We take them off their mothers' milk and wean them on alfalfa hay, prairie hay, and a ration of grain. While they are around the corrals during this weaning period, we may want to run them through the chute and give them an age brand. If the year is 1975, we brand them with a 5 on the side or shoulder where it will show up. In years to come, we can determine each animal's age at a glance. And while we have the heifers in the chute, we might also want to clean up the horns—remove the snaggle horns that often grow back after an animal has been dehorned the first time. Snaggle horns sometimes curl around and grow into the animal's head, so it is a good idea to clean up the horns while we have the opportunity. We might also want to give them a "calfhood" vaccination, which will give them lifetime immunity to bangs.

We keep them up in the weaning pen for two weeks. When they have settled down, begun to eat, and have stopped bawling for their mommas, we will turn them out into a pasture by themselves. We don't want to expose them to a bull at this point, and that is why we keep them isolated. Heifers can be pasture-bred (bred accidentally while they are still with their mothers) when they are still quite small. While some ranchers don't mind this, there is a school of thought that holds that if heifers are bred too soon they will never reach their full growth, and that they will have more problems delivering their first calf than heifers that are allowed to grow and mature. So we keep them separated and don't expose them to a bull. We take them through the winter, through the summer, and through another winter. Then, in June of their third year, when they are past-two-year-olds, we turn a bull in with them.

Why June? Well, we know that the gestation period for cattle is about nine months. If we breed them in June, they will start calving the following March. By March, the worst of the winter weather should be over and they won't be calving in ice and snow.

The kind of bull we choose to put with them is important, and we will have given a lot of thought to this decision. First-calf heifers are a special case, and rules of breeding which would normally apply to pasture cows do not necessarily apply to heifers. With pasture cows, you breed for growth and size. You want big calves that will push down on the scales on shipping day. With first-calf heifers, you want just the opposite—a small, thin-hipped calf that a heifer can deliver without complications. You don't care if the heifer's calf is sorry-looking. Most heifers' calves are sorry-looking anyway, because the heifers don't give enough milk to raise a big, sappy calf. Calving out heifers is the science of guiding a young female and her calf through the most dangerous period they will ever face, and this is upmost in your mind when you choose your heifer bull.

Let's say that our heifers are of the Hereford breed. Prevailing wisdom holds that we should mate them with a bull of a smaller breed. Simmental, Charolais, and Santa Gertrudis cattle are all larger than Herefords, so, according to the prevailing wisdom, these breeds will not make good heifer bulls. What about a Hereford bull on Hereford heifers? Some say this works and others say it causes problems that can be avoided if you go to a smaller, thinner, lighter-boned breed. Black Angus are popular as heifer bulls. Some people use Jersey bulls, arguing that this milk breed produces a small, thin calf that shoots right out. Others will make the same claim about Brangus, Brahman, and Brahman-cross bulls.

One of the most interesting developments in the cattle business in recent years is the revival of the longhorn breed and the increasing use of longhorn bulls on first-calf heifers. As everyone knows, the old longhorn was the primary beef-producing animal in the United States between about 1865 and 1880. The breed was tough and self-sufficient. Herds of longhorns could be assembled in South Texas and driven up the trail to railheads in Kansas, and if properly handled, they could actually gain weight along the way. But when the trail-driving days passed into history, when windmills and barbed wire fences opened up the vast western prairies to ranching, and when ranching began to evolve into a systematic business of converting grass into pounds of beef, the longhorn was replaced by British breeds, which were not as hardy, but which carried more flesh. Early in this century, the longhorn suffered such a decline in popularity that it came very close to extinction. Ranchers may have enjoyed reading about the old longhorn, but they certainly didn't want any in their breeding herds.

But the more highly bred cattle carried an intrinsic weakness: the more they were bred for size and a beef-producing carcass, the more difficulty the heifers had in delivering their first calves. Then, ten or fifteen years ago, it occurred to some bright fellow that calving problems did not exist among the longhorns, any more than they existed among wild animals. Having escaped from Spanish explorers in the New World, the longhorns had lived in the wild long before American cowboys began to round them up out of the brush and send them up the trail. Nature had taken care of the calving problems of the longhorn through natural selection, and here was a gene pool that seemed ideally suited to solving the calving problems of the over-civilized British breeds.

As a result of this and other factors, the longhorn breed is making an impressive return from the edge of extinction, and longhorn bulls are being actively promoted as ideal bulls for first-calf heifers. I have talked with ranchers who have used them, and they were impressed with the results. If what you read and hear is true, the longhorn is working himself back into a job and may be around for a long time to come.

But longhorn bulls are still something of a curiosity in our part of the country and are hard to find, so let's turn three small Brangus bulls in with our heifers. Summer comes and goes, then fall, then winter. Along about the middle of February, we gather the heifers and look them over in the corral. We cut off five heavy springers (those which are close to calving) and haul them to the heifer trap near the house. We will keep them there and check them four or five times a day until they calve. A heavy springer will often be as round as a little barrel, she will be making a milk bag, and her genitalia will have begun to show signs of swelling.

Now that we have springing heifers around the place, our daily routine changes, and supervising them becomes a high-priority job. First thing in the morning, we drive or ride out into the trap and look them over, and every three or four hours we check them again.

Let's say that one day right after lunch we notice that one of them is acting strangely. She has gone off to herself. She is holding her tail out and she seems restless. She lies down, then she stands up and walks, then lies down again. She is going into labor. We mark the time: one o'clock. We will check her again in an hour. When we return, she is lying on the ground, and we see a little pair of hooves showing beneath her tail. She has begun delivery and so far there is nothing to indicate that she might be having trouble. We will leave her alone for another forty-five minutes, in hopes that she will deliver the calf herself. It is always better to let nature do its own work, and we will intrude only if it becomes necessary. When we check her again forty-five minutes later, she is on her feet and licking a newborn calf.

That makes one down and only forty-nine to go. We will keep her in the heifer trap for a week, until we are certain that she has cleaned (sloughed the afterbirth and avoided the infection that can result if she doesn't), and that she has accepted the calf as her own (some heifers are so ignorant of mothering that they won't claim their own calf or let it nurse). Then we will turn the pair out into the pasture with the other cows.

The next four heifers calve out just as easily as the first one, and we turn them out into the pasture. We bring ten more springers to the house, turn them into the heifer trap, and begin watching them. By this time, we are feeling pretty good about this heifer crop. Calving problems seem to run in cycles. One year you won't have any trouble at all, and the next you will have all the problems you want. Why? Nobody knows. Sandy Hagar on the YL Ranch, who taught me more about heifers than anyone else, used to say, "I've been calving out heifers all my life, and every year I know less about them than I did before." Pregnant heifers have their own peculiar ways of humbling a cowboy. Just when you think you've learned all the signs and can predict what a heifer is going to do, she will make a monkey out of you. The heifer you watch closely, thinking that she will calve any minute, will go another three weeks without having a calf, while the small, thin one that you think is a month away will suddenly go into labor. Sandy had come up with only one infallible rule for picking the heaviest heifer out of a bunch: she's the one that calved last night.

We have calved out five heifers and we think this is going to be one of those good years. Thoughts of a fool.

The next morning at seven o'clock we make our routine check on the girls in the heifer trap, and we find three of them on the ground and in labor. We checked them last night at dark and knew, *knew* that they were all a week away from calving. Well, so much for our understanding of heifers. Since we don't know when they started labor, we have to assume the worst, that they started in the night and are having trouble. We saddle a horse and ride out. We get them up and drive all three into the corral, cut out one and drive her into a narrow alley where we can restrain her. (A cow-sized doctoring chute works fine for this until you get a heifer that becomes so weak that she falls down; then you have the problem of how to get her out of the chute before she chokes to death on the head gate.) While she is standing in the alley, we go to the barn for our equipment: a plastic bucket, warm water, antiseptic-lubricant, calf-pulling chains, and a set of come-alongs, or fence-stretchers.

We strip down to a T-shirt and wash our hands and arms in the solution of water and antiseptic. Then we work our hands into the heifer's vagina and grope around until we feel the calf's head and feet. In the normal and correct position, an unborn calf will have its head facing the outside, chin side down, with a front foot on each side of the head. That's what we find. Everything is in the correct position, and we know that the heifer has just been unable to get the calf out. Maybe the calf is too large in the shoulders. Maybe the heifer is too small in the hips. Maybe she had just started labor when we found her and hasn't had enough time to finish the job. But we can't take any chances. Once the water bag has been broken and the delivery process has begun, the calf's life is in danger.

We get the pulling chain out of the water, make a loop in one end, reach inside the heifer, and fit the loop above the hock of the calf's front leg. Then we hook the other end of the chain to the other leg. We connect the stretchers to the bottom of a post, so that we will be pulling at a downward angle, and start taking up the slack. As we apply pressure, the heifer begins to strain along with us. The calf's head pops free. The shoulders clear. The hips pass, and the wet, slimy little creature comes tumbling out on the ground. It blinks its eyes and takes its first gurgle of air. We carry the calf into a pen and drive the heifer in with it. If we are lucky, she will claim the calf and begin licking it dry, and when it can stand, she will allow it to nurse.

We still have two more heifers lined up, so we bring another one up and run her into the alley. We reach into her body and discover the problem: one of the calf's front legs has gotten turned around. We have to go deeper and feel around until we find the leg. There isn't much working space inside a heifer, and every time she is seized by a contraction, it mashes our hand against her pelvic bone. Sometimes it hurts. But we find the leg and bring it up into the correct position. We put on the chains and start jacking on the come-along. This is a bull calf, and since bulls are larger at birth than heifers, they are more difficult to deliver. This one just doesn't want to come out. We've got his head out, but he's hung up in the shoulders. Again, we jack on the come-along and apply terrible pressure on the heifer. She strains and groans. We think we're going to pull her guts out, but we can't quit. If we stop and think the situation over, the calf may die. So we jack some more on the come-along. Then we stand on the cable and jump up and down. At last the shoulders clear.

The heifer bawls and staggers. She thinks it's over, but it's not. The calf hangs in the hips. We take the slack out of the stretcher and jack it until it is as tight as we can make it. Once again, we stand on the cable and jump up and down, gaining an inch every time our weight comes down. Finally the calf pops out and hits the ground, and we fall on top of him. Hearing a strange commotion behind her, the heifer kicks us squarely in the back.

Well, it's done. The calf looks up at us and utters its first "maaaaa." He'll be sore for a few days, but he's alive and so is the heifer. The operation was a success. We clear the alley and go for the third heifer.

We know at first glance that this is going to be a bad one. This heifer's calf is already dead and its head is swollen. The heifer must have started labor right after we checked her at dark last night. When a calf dies inside its mother, decomposition sets in at once and the carcass begins to swell and inflate with gasses. In this swollen state, it won't exit the heifer's body. We know what must be done, and it isn't very pleasant. We dig out our pocket knife and slit the calf's throat. When we apply pressure with the come-along, fluids and gasses can escape through the cut, making the calf's body small enough to pass to the outside. Sometimes you have to remove the entire head, and I have heard of instances where the calf had to be dismembered and removed in pieces. In a case this extreme, a veterinarian would perform a Caesarean section, but that operation is beyond the skills of the ordinary cowboy.

We hook up the chains and go to work. We jack and we pull and we strain and we jump on the cable. The calf is lost, but we must try to save the heifer.

By now, the poor beast is so exhausted and weak that she falls down. She bawls in pain, but we must keep pulling on the calf. We can hear things squish and pop inside her. We don't see how she can survive this horrible abuse. It goes on for half an hour, until we finally get the calf out. The heifer lets out a gasp and her head falls to the ground. Panting, covered with blood and gore, we lean against the fence. This is one of the low points in a cowboy's experience. After he has done his best to save the heifer and has put her through agony, it appears that he has killed her.

But fifteen minutes later she is still breathing. After another fifteen minutes, she raises her head. We leave her in the alley for two hours and let her rest. When we come back, her eyes are sunken and she looks terrible, but she is still alive. We have to get her up and moving around, so we prod her until she staggers to her feet. In this situation, when a cowboy must get a weakened animal to its feet, some fellows place their hands over the animal's nostrils and cut off its wind. In struggling for breath, the critter will regain its feet. Other cowboys will throw snuff or spit tobacco juice into its eyes, which often brings the animal to life. This sounds harsh, but there is no easy or polite way of getting a seven- or eight-hundred-pound beast to its feet.

The heifer is very weak and partially paralyzed in her back legs. We'll keep her up in the corral and watch her. She'll live, but she may be partially paralyzed for the rest of her life. If she's still gimped-up in two or three months, we'll probably take her to town and sell her. A cow that is weak or crippled in the hind legs cannot stand up when a bull tries to mount her. If he can't mount her, he can't breed her, which means that she will remain barren and unproductive.

Every now and then you run across a heifer that will not accept her calf. She doesn't have the mothering instinct, and she reminds you of a teenager who doesn't want to be tied down and wants to get back to having a good time. This kind of heifer will not lick her calf and might even run from it. If she were out in the pasture, she would leave it to die. If she's in a corral, the calf will follow her around and try to nurse. The heifer will run, kick, and butt the poor little thing and do everything she can to keep it away from her. After a cowboy has pulled the calf and brought it safely into the world, he's not about to let the heifer get by with this nonsense. He puts her and her calf into a small pen where the heifer can't escape. If she continues to kick the calf away, the cowboy takes stronger measures. Sandy Hagar used to stand in the pen with a club, and every time the heifer took a shot at her calf, old Sandy gave her a good whack. In his twenty years on the YL Ranch, he used this technique to introduce many a silly heifer to the joys of parenthood.

Another way you can deal with this problem is to run the heifer into a cow chute and squeeze her down so that she can't move or kick. Then you carry the calf up to the chute, squirt some milk into his mouth, and hold him there until he starts nursing. Once he's gotten the taste of warm milk, he goes to work, sucking out every quarter and butting old Ma with his nose. The heifer will try to kick him off, and often she bawls in protest, but there is nothing she can do about it. Usually, after you've run the heifer into the chute three or four times, she accepts the calf and stops fighting it. But not always. In 1978 I had a heifer that was determined that she wasn't going to be a mother. I whacked on her with a club, I ran her through the chute three times a day, and she still bullied her calf. She had the calf so thoroughly intimidated that it wouldn't go near her unless she was in the chute. I solved the problem by putting a pair of horse hobbles on her hind legs. I left the hobbles on for a month and turned the pair out into the pasture, and finally the heifer gave up and stopped kicking.

When a heifer loses her calf, the cowboy can try to "graft" or " 'dopt" another cow's calf onto her. Once again, he must reach into his bag of tricks to help the adoption along. A cow brute identifies her calf by smell, and she has a natural instinct to shun any strange-smelling critter that tries to nurse. To get around this, the cowboy might skin out the heifer's dead calf and tie the skin on the adoptee. When the heifer smells the new calf for the first time, it has the right scent and she lets it nurse. By the time the skin falls off, she has usually accepted the calf as her own. Or the cowboy can spray the new calf with deodorant, such as Right Guard, and then spray some of it into the heifer's nose. This confuses her sense of smell, and she will often accept the calf.

Calving out heifers is an important part of the cowboy's job. It isn't glamorous, it isn't romantic, and you'll never see it in a John Wayne movie. And that's probably a good thing. What goes on in heifer-calving season is not the stuff from which legends are made.

PART FOUR: THE BOTTOM LINE

16
The Modern Cattle Business

Many colorful character-types entered the drama of American history and then disappeared when economic conditions changed. The fur trapper, the Indian trader, the buffalo hunter, the gold prospector, the riverboat pilot, and the trail driver all made glorious but brief appearances on the western stage. Not one of these characters exists today, and their demise can be explained in simple economic terms: they disappeared when their professions ceased to be profitable ventures.

Compared to the trail driver and the buffalo hunter, whose golden ages lasted about a decade, the cowboy is a durable figure. Since he has lasted a hundred years through good times and bad, we might be tempted to say that he is immune to the laws of economics and that he will always be with us. That may or may not be true. The working cowboy (as opposed to the "urban cowboy" or the cowboy-as-legend) functions in an economic milieu: ranching, which is the business of raising beef cattle for a profit. If ranching ever disappears from the scene, the working cowboy will go with it. Any discussion of the modern cowboy would be incomplete without some mention of ranch economics and a look at the bottom line.

We should begin by distinguishing between a farm and a ranch. The term *farming* implies cultivation—plowing, planting, and harvesting crops—and

The basic raw material in a ranch operation is grass, and cattle ranching is the business of converting grass into beef.

a patch of cultivated land is called a field. The word *ranch* implies grassland, which is not plowed or planted or harvested, and a patch of ranchland is called a pasture. As a general rule, the farmer raises crops and the rancher raises livestock.

The basic raw material in a ranch operation is grass, and cattle ranching is the business of converting grass into beef. This miracle of changing coarse roughage into delicious beefsteak is performed in the four-chambered stomach of a bovine animal. When we eat a broiled steak, we are, to a large degree, eating grass that has been chemically altered.

The cattle business operates on several levels, and the first is the cow-calf operation. All beef cattle originate on a cow-calf ranch. At this end of the business, the rancher runs mother cows on pastureland. A small rancher in the plains country might keep a hundred or two hundred brood cows; a large ranch might have as many as five thousand. Under normal conditions, a cow will produce a calf every year for about nine years. Revenue from a cow-calf operation derives from the sale of the yearly calf crop, when the calves are shipped and sold at a weight between four and five hundred pounds.

From that point, the calves enter the stocker or yearling end of the business. There are two types of yearling operations: those that winter light cattle on wheat and oat pasture, and those that summer them on grass. In both cases the yearling operator buys light cattle (around four hundred) and tries to put as much weight on them as possible. When he sells them, they have reached feeder weight (six hundred or seven hundred pounds), and most feeder cattle go to a feedlot, where they will receive a finishing ration that will take them up to slaughter weight (between nine hundred and twelve hundred pounds).

The beef chain starts here, with a good old mother cow and her calf on a ranch. The old tires in the background were used to control wind erosion in sandhills where a pipeline went through the country.

Certain regions of the country have proved better for summer grazing than for year-round grazing in a cow-calf operation. The Flint Hills of Kansas, the Osage region of Oklahoma, and the rolling ranch country in northeastern New Mexico all have the reputation of being steer country and are used by yearling operators who stock the pastures in the spring, take full advantage of the strong summer grasses, and then pull out at the end of the growing season in the fall.

Before about 1960, feeder-weight steers were either slaughtered right off Flint Hills or Osage grass or else shipped to the Midwest corn belt for fattening. But in the years since 1960, the focus of the feeding industry has moved from the Midwest to California, Arizona, and the high plains region of Texas, Oklahoma, and Kansas. In 1980, the major cattle-feeding region in the United States is located within a 120-mile radius of Amarillo, Texas. This shift was directly related to the rise of irrigated farming in the high plains region, which yields large quantities of feed grains that are the basic ingredient in any cattle-feeding operation.

In a feedlot, large numbers of cattle (up to sixty thousand head) are concentrated in a small area, confined to pens, and fed a concentrated ration of grain until they reach slaughter weight. At this point they are called "fats," or fat cattle, and are purchased at the feedlot by buyers from packing houses. Twenty years ago, the big names in the packing industry were Swift, Armour, and Wilson, and their operations were centered in the Midwest. Today, the packing industry is undergoing changes. The old, established packers in the Midwest are phasing out their beef operations and concentrating on pork, while the beef end of the business has been taken over by younger companies, such as Monfort, Iowa Beef, and Missouri Beef, which are locating their facilities closer to the feedlots in Texas, Oklahoma, and Colorado.

That is a quick survey of the cattle business from top to bottom. What I have presented here is a rough and general outline. There are exceptions at every stage, but it isn't necessary to go into them. Now let's back up and take a closer look at the cow-calf operator and study his approach to the cattle business in more detail.

Cow-calf operators fall into two categories: the registered breeder and the commercial breeder. The registered breeder is not raising animals for slaughter, but rather he is the source of purebred breeding stock. He keeps careful records on every animal in his herd and follows a program of scientific breeding that will produce animals with superior genetic qualities. There are many qualities that he tries to introduce into his herd, but ultimately there is only one that matters: pounds of beef against cost of gain. When the commercial cowman wants to improve and upgrade his herd, he goes to a purebred stock operator, studies the bloodlines and the results of various tests that have been conducted, and buys the improved stock that he needs and can afford. Purebred stock is expensive, but it is usually a sound investment.

The ordinary rancher falls into the category of commercial breeder. He tries to maintain a good herd of cows and is constantly trying to upgrade his breeding stock by bringing in purebred animals from the outside. If he did not do this, if he drew all his breeding animals from his own herd, over a period of years his cattle would become inbred and suffer from genetic fatigue. Calves raised on a commercial operation will usually go to slaughter, though if the rancher has a good reputation as a breeder, he may sell a few bulls here and there, and his heifers may bring a premium price, selling as brood animals rather than for slaughter.

There are dozens of beef breeds, and each has its strong points, its national association that keeps records on bloodlines and registration, and its group of enthusiastic supporters. When ranchers of Charles Goodnight's generation first began upgrading their cow herds, they brought in breeds from the British Isles: Herefords, Angus, and Durhams. These cattle were more efficient at converting grass into beef than the longhorn, and they proved themselves in other areas that were important to the cattle raiser: they did well under range conditions, the cows made good mothers, the bulls covered their territory and did their job, and, with supplemental feeding, the British breeds could tolerate severe winter weather.

But in the 1950s cattlemen began to take a second look at the British cattle. For all their proven advantages, they were too small. If a rancher ran heavier cattle, couldn't he produce more pounds of beef and increase the income of his ranch operation? In response to this interest in heavier weaning weights in calves, breeders began to import larger types of cattle from Europe: Charolais, Simmental, Limousin, Main-Anjou, Chianina, Marchigiana, Blonde d'Aquitaine, and others. These "exotic" breeds did not replace the British breeds as all-purpose ranch stock, but were used primarily in crossbreeding programs.

Crossbreeding is an attempt by the rancher to increase his production of beef through genetics rather than by external expansion (the purchase of more land). The offspring of a crossbreeding program not only acquire greater size from one of the parent animals, but also are stimulated by heterosis, or "hybrid vigor." If a rancher owned a herd of good Hereford cows and wanted to increase the size and weaning weights of his calf crop, he might attend the sale at a registered Charolais operation and buy several bulls. Out of the Hereford-Charolais cross, he would get a heavier calf that, in theory, would bring in more dollars to the operation. Some cattlemen have gone beyond the first crossing and have used second and third crosses. I know a rancher in Oklahoma who breeds Hereford cows to Angus bulls to produce a black baldface calf. From this first cross he saves the heifers, grows them to cows, and breeds them to a Brangus bull. He considers the calf from this second crossing a superior beef animal, better than the Hereford, Angus, or Brangus breed.

Crossbreeding affects only the offspring, but some cattlemen have sustained the crossbreeding process over a period of years for the very purpose of creating new breeds of cattle, breeds that they feel are superior in certain ways to existing breeds. One of the most famous new breeds is the Santa Gertrudis, which was developed on the King Ranch in Texas. Shorthorn and Brahman cattle were crossbred, then inbred until the genetic factors stabilized at five-eighths shorthorn and three-eighths Brahman, producing an animal that was ideally suited to the climate and conditions found on the King Ranch in South Texas. Brangus, another new (1946) breed, combines three-eighths Brahman and five-eighths Angus. The Beefmaster, developed by Tom Lasater on a ranch near Falfurrias, Texas, combines one-half Brahman, one-fourth shorthorn, and one-fourth Hereford. And every year the list of new breeds grows longer: Charbray (Charolais × Brahman), Brahmental (Brahman × Simmental), Red Brangus (Red Angus × Brahman), Simbrah (Simmental × Brahman), and others. Some of these new breeds have not been around long enough to establish themselves and are not often seen outside the herds of a few pureblood stock breeders. Others, such as the Brangus, Santa Gertrudis, and Beefmaster, have become mainline breeds and can now be found on ranches all over the world.

With the growing interest in recent years in the longhorn breed, I predict that eventually someone will develop a new breed of cattle from a crossing between longhorns and one of the major British breeds, and if I were a cattleman I would be interested in this crossing. If you could incorporate the strength of the longhorn—natural resistance to disease and insects, no calving problems, durability, and the ability of these cattle to gain weight on low quality roughage and to go through the winter without supplemental feeding—with the carcass quality of the Hereford, it seems to me you would have a breed that couldn't be beat.

The British breeds adapted well to the climate and range conditions in higher elevations and drier climates, say, from the Texas South Plains up to the Canadian border. Along the Mexican border and the Gulf Coast, in South Texas, the Deep South, and southeastern states, they did not fare so well, and cattlemen had to find breeds with more tolerance to heat and more natural resistance to ticks, parasites, and diseases. They found the right kind of cattle in the Indian Brahman and the Brazilian Zebu, and today a high percentage of cattle found in hot, humid climates are either Brahman-type animals or new breeds with a high percentage of Brahman blood.

American cattlemen have been the most innovative stockmen in the entire world. They have traveled all over the globe to find established breeds that would fill a particular need or solve a particular problem, and when better breeds of cattle could not be found, they developed new ones. Since the cattle business began a little more than a century ago, American ranchers have continued to improve and upgrade their livestock, to produce more pounds of beef per acre of land, and to provide the consumer with the best and cheapest beef on earth.

17

Economics and the Rancher

Over the years ranchers have tried to operate in a climate of simple textbook economics. A man owns some land. He works hard, manages his stock carefully, and produces a commodity which the American consumer wants: beef. Because he deals in a supply-and-demand market, there will be years of high supply, low demand, and low prices, and in these years he might only break even or lose money. But there will be other years, when the trend will be reversed, and he will make a profit. Over a ten-year period, he can expect the good years and bad years to average out so that he comes out ahead of the game. In theory, this type of free market economy will reward thrift, good management, and hard work and will weed out marginal operators who don't tend to their business. Cattlemen have accepted the risks and rewards of the free market system and have resisted the introduction of artificial restraints and rewards into it.

But the economic climate has changed in recent years, and people in the cattle business are having a hard time adjusting to it. In the first place, ranchers have begun to suspect that the *free* market system is not so free any more, and that it can be—and has been—manipulated by politicians in Washington, who have figured out that 96 percent of the voters in the United States are food consumers instead of food producers. These con-

Oil and gas income is the dirty little secret of the modern cattle business.

sumers pay the smallest percentage of their after-tax income for food of any people in the world (slightly less than 15 percent in 1975), and they have come to regard cheap food as a constitutional right. They are encouraged to think this way by politicians who speak of "our" wheat and "our" livestock, as though agricultural products were natural resources owned jointly by the people, and who promise to do something about the rising cost of groceries. If you happen to be running for public office, it's good business to promise cheap food. You may outrage 4 percent of the voters (farmers and ranchers), but you will win the approval of the 96 percent who have nothing to lose and everything to gain.

In 1973 when retail beef prices hit an all-time high, consumer groups in the East began a protest movement against high prices and organized a boycott on beef. Naturally, the beef boycott was not popular among cattlemen, but they recognized that such an action was a legitimate part of the free market system. When prices reach high levels, consumer resistance appears. Demand diminishes, supplies increase, and prices begin to fall. That's the way the system is supposed to work. But in 1973 the federal government stepped in. To win the approval of urban voters, the Nixon administration imposed a price ceiling on beef at the retail level, thereby introducing an artificial restraint into the marketing system. All at once livestock prices were no longer responding to supply and demand, but instead to President Nixon's commandment that retail beef was only worth so much per pound. Cattlemen were thrown into confusion. They didn't know how to respond. Many of them held cattle in the feedlots, thinking that Nixon would soon lift the price ceiling and spare them from losing money.

They were wrong. Cattle held in the feedlots were overfed and overfinished, which not only decreased their quality and value, but increased the supply of beef. By the time the price freeze was lifted, it had achieved its purpose: feedlots had finished cattle stacked from fence to fence, and the industry found itself grossly overstocked and oversupplied. President Nixon had broken the beef market with the stroke of a pen. He had also issued a warning to cattle producers—no modern president, even one who fancies himself a fiscal conservative, can allow the laws of supply and demand to operate against the interests of 96 percent of the electorate.

Nixon's price freeze on beef was just another headline in urban papers. It was invoked, it was lifted, and it was soon forgotten by the urban consumer. But in the cattle business it produced an economic earthquake that shook the industry from top to bottom. In just a matter of months, the price of stocker cattle coming off the ranches plunged to 50 percent of its previous level. Yearling operators who had bought calves in the fall for a dollar a pound saw their net worth cut in half and found themselves looking at a guaranteed loss of fifty or sixty dollars a head. And the cattle feeders who had held their fat cattle in the lots, hoping for higher prices, finally had to sell for whatever they could get, sometimes taking losses of two hundred dollars a head. The losses were staggering. Many feedlots, including Wheatheart Feeders, one of the largest feeding operations in the world, went into bankruptcy. Many yearling operators were driven out of business, and many of those who survived are still carrying the debt they incurred in that one year. Today, six years later, they are hanging on, hoping for a good year, and financing their debt at 12 percent to 20 percent interest.

Several observers have pointed out that the cattle business had already reached a point of oversupply by the fall of 1973, and that the market would have fallen on its own even if Nixon had not imposed the price freeze. That may be true. But under free market conditions, the price of cattle would have declined gradually and stockmen would have had time to adjust to the change. Nixon's action simply turned the natural braking mechanism of the market into a derailment and a wreck.

Anyone who was involved in the cattle business between 1973 and 1978 learned a painful lesson he will not soon forget. He learned that the federal government is committed to a policy of cheap food and that it will not allow cattlemen to make profits which, in the vernacular of the consumer, are "obscene," even if those obscene profits are needed to pay off debts at the bank. Nowadays, when a stockman buys cattle, he has to worry not only about death loss, disease, drought, blizzards, and acts of God, but also about what his government in Washington might do to him. Cattlemen used to worry when cattle prices began to fall. Today, they worry when prices rise too quickly. They have a genuine fear that the government, through either edict or manipulation of beef imports, will step in to break the market again.

No president since Nixon has imposed a price ceiling on beef, but the threat is there, lurking in the background, and a threat is just as good as an overt action. Cattlemen know that any president, regardless of his party or his political philosophy, will throttle the livestock industry any time the need arises. To keep the government out of the cattle business, stockmen have tried to restrain their own markets and to avoid sudden escalations in price that might bring consumers to a new boil.

One result of this psychological price fixing is that cattle raising has become a poor investment. When you consider the investment-return ratio, the risk, and the amount of labor involved in cattle raising, you wonder why anyone would knowingly walk into the business. That's a very interesting question, and there are two answers to it. The first is that old-time ranching families are in the business because they like it and don't want to do anything else. Ranching is their way of life. Others—newcomers, new money, investors, corporations—are coming into ranching for entirely different reasons, which we will examine later on.

A second economic force that confronts the modern cattleman is inflation, the same inexorable ante-up that is causing anxiety and dislocation throughout our economy. But inflation is particularly burdensome to the cattleman because, unlike most businessmen, he cannot pass along his higher cost of operation to someone else. The truckers can. The packers can. The supermarkets can. But the cattleman can't. He must take whatever the market offers, and while cattle prices have risen a great deal since the dark days of 1974 and 1975, so have the costs of operation: pickups, trailers, gasoline, parts, leather, veterinary medicine, taxes, and interest. Whatever the cattleman has gained in cattle prices he has lost to inflation, so that his financial position has improved little or not at all over the past seven years. Once again, it is hard to escape the feeling that nobody but a fool would invest in cattle.

But here is an irony: despite the hardship inflation has brought to cattlemen, it has kept many of them in business and out of bankruptcy. How? During periods of inflation, when the government printing presses are running twenty-four hours a day to turn out increasingly worthless dollars, investors seek out commodities with real or intrinsic value: gold, silver, antiques, art, real estate, and land. As they say, "God ain't making any more land." Land is real. You can walk on it, see it, feel it, build a house on it. The value of agricultural land has been rising steadily over the past ten years—an increase that has nothing whatever to do with its productive capacity (which remains the same from year to year) or its potential for generating income (which, in the case of cattle, remains dismal). Farm and ranch land is in-

A rancher was once asked what he would do if he were given a million dollars. He thought about it for a moment, then said, "I guess I'd stay in the cattle business til I went through it and then I'd go look for another job." Like the cowboy, the rancher is devoted to a way of life that can be demanding and frustrating. But it also has its rewards.

creasing in value because investors *think it is valuable*—period. No one who buys Texas Panhandle grassland today at two hundred dollars an acre can hope to pay it off with cattle. Cattle wouldn't even pay the interest on the loan. The value of two-hundred-dollar-an-acre grass is strictly theoretical, and it derives from inflation.

The importance of inflated land prices to the cattleman is that, even though he can't make a living raising cattle, his net worth keeps jumping up from year to year, as the value of his land continues to rise against paper dollars, thereby increasing the size of his collateral and enabling him to borrow more money at the bank in order to continue his operation. At the same time, his debt at the bank is slowly melting away, as each dollar he borrowed in 1974 loses eight to thirteen cents in value every year due to inflation. This is a house of cards and an economic Land of Oz, but it is the situation many ranchers find themselves in. Had inflation not made them paper millionaires, they would have been out of business years ago.

Thus far, I have painted a grim picture of modern ranch economics, yet in certain respects my description of the situation does not mesh with observable facts. For example, if you look at the four-color ads in a livestock magazine or breed journal, the impression you come away with is not one of extreme poverty or hardship for ranching. The *articles* might dwell on hard times and low prices, but the *ads* tell a different story. They tell of high-powered breeder sales at ranches out in West Texas that have airstrips long enough to accommodate Lear Jets and King-airs. They tell of exotic bulls selling for one or two hundred thousand dollars, and of registered quarter horses that fetch prices in the same range. "If this is how ranchers behave when they're going broke," you say to yourself, "we should all be going broke in the cattle business."

Being a rancher ain't much fun when you're wading in mud, a cold rain is dripping off your hat, and your cattle are losing weight.

Obviously there is more than one side to the economics of modern ranching, and some of the folks seem to be doing very well indeed. But we should keep one fact in mind: the modern cattle baron did not make his fortune in cattle, at least not recently. If he has money, it is old money made by Grandpa and passed along, or oil and gas money that comes from producing wells on the ranch, or it is outside money looking for a tax loophole, an inflation hedge, or the kind of solid respectability that comes from owning a ranch in Texas.

Oil and gas income is the dirty little secret of the modern cattle business. No one wants to talk about it, perhaps because ranchers prefer to think of themselves as self-made men and are uncomfortable with the knowledge that they have managed to get something for nothing. The trade journals and papers rarely discuss oil and gas income. The subject of an article on ranching will go on at length about his new fencing program, his new brush-clearance program, his new breeding program, his new barns and so forth, and the uninitiated reader might very well come away thinking that this fellow is an outstanding manager who is doing things as they ought to be done. People in the business know better. They understand that, in this day and age, cattle don't buy new barns or new anything, that this fellow is improving his ranch with outside money, and that the secret to his good management probably lies in the fifteen producing wells out in his pastures. Everybody in the business knows it, yet no one will come out and talk about it. I don't know why ranchers should be ashamed of their oil and gas income. After all, had the cattle business not been subsidized by this outside money, the entire industry might have gone under after the market wreck of 1974–75.

Another type of prosperous rancher these days is the doctor, lawyer, dentist, movie star, or oil magnate who has made a fortune in another line of work and buys a ranch. He goes into ranching for one of several reasons. On the advice of his financial advisers, he might be looking for a long-term, inflation-proof investment, in which case he may find ranch property more attractive than condominiums or shopping centers. Or he may be looking for a tax write-off, a semilegitimate business that will give his accountants some leverage to use against the tax collector. Or he might just want to play rancher on weekends and holidays and have a place to hunt deer and quail in the fall. But there is one thing you can be sure of: he doesn't go into ranching with the idea of making money on cattle. He won't, and he knows it.

This type of rancher enjoys the best of both worlds. He can partake of the ranching way of life, yet he doesn't have to make a living at it. Typically, his ranch is a showplace, with handsome barns, new corrals, painted fence around the horse pasture, blooded horses, registered cattle, and a college-educated hired hand who owns the title of "herdsman."

The introduction of outside money into the cattle business has created the impression of false prosperity and is distorting ranch economics at a fundamental level. When outside interests invest in ranch land and dabble in exotic cattle, they often subsidize management concepts that have nothing whatever to do with profit and loss. The ranch becomes a toy. It is immune to the laws of economics, and once again we find ourselves in the Land of Oz, where ranchers appear to be rolling in dough but are raising cattle at a loss. The cattle business is being propped up by outside money, the real cattle producers are either going out of business or hanging on because of land appreciation, and the consumer, who keeps complaining about the price of beef, is buying a subsidized product that is a good deal cheaper than it ought to be. If all the subsidies were suddenly removed from the cattle business tomorrow—corporate money, oil and gas money, doctor-lawyer money—beef and cattle prices would have to rise or the entire industry would be thrown into turmoil.

In our post—World War II prosperity we Americans became accustomed to cheap energy and cheap food, and we have built a consumer society based on these two cornerstones. The OPEC nations have informed us that energy is no longer cheap, and the time may be coming when we have to learn the same lesson about agricultural products.

18
Economics and the Cowboy

Much of what we know about the American cowboy comes from the recollections of men who cowboyed in their youth but then went on to better things. Teddy Blue Abbott married the daughter of Granville Stuart and became a rancher in Montana. Will Rogers went into show business. Charlie Russell became a famous artist, sculptor, and illustrator. Ben K. Green practiced veterinary medicine. Philip Ashton Rollins, J. Frank Dobie, Walter Prescott Webb, and Edward Everett Dale chose the route of scholarship and university teaching. Ramon Adams was a businessman in Dallas, and a fellow named Teddy Roosevelt became president of the United States. All these men wrote books about cowboying. They captured the romance, adventure, excitement, and humor of the cowboy's life—all the qualities that appeal to young men and draw them toward the horseback life.

Yet none of these men grew old in the saddle, had to support a family on cowboy wages, or had to face the autumn of life without a pension or shelter. This has created a blind spot in the literature of the West. That blind spot centers on the poverty in which cowboys have lived and on their financial dealings with their employers. It is not enough to pass over this subject with little homilies about the "honor" of being a cowboy, and it is neither fair nor accurate to romanticize the poverty of the cowboy. Western writers never

"Honey, if the boss could afford to pay me better, I know that he would."

seem to tire of pointing out that cowboys were overworked and underpaid, but no one ever seems to wonder why. Did ranchers think that too much money would corrupt their cowboys? Were the cowboys so devoted to romantic poverty that they turned down better wages?

Cowboying has always been a very demanding, low paying profession. It was that way from the very beginning of the cattle business, and over the years it has been frozen by tradition. Today, when a young man chooses the horseback life, he knows that he won't make any money at it. To an outsider, the low wages might imply that cowboying is a profession that demands few skills and little intelligence, yet we have seen that this is not the case. The cowboy is every bit as skilled and competent in his field as any plumber, electrician, or carpenter. He just doesn't get paid as much for it. In the cattle business, tradition holds that you should pay top dollar for herd bulls and stud horses and bottom dollar for cowboys, and this rule has applied in the good years as well as during the bad.

There is no mystery as to why ranchers have followed this tradition. If you are a businessman, especially in a high-risk enterprise such as cattle raising, you cut costs where you can and pay no more for goods and services than you have to. That's the way you make a profit and stay in business. If a rancher can hire cowboys for six hundred dollars a month, why should he offer seven hundred dollars or eight hundred dollars? Of course you could turn the question around and argue the other side: if the rancher is prospering and making money on the ranch, why *shouldn't* he pay seven hundred dollars or eight hundred dollars to the men who have cared for his stock and property; why *shouldn't* he reward them in a good year, instead of making donations to the church, the local library, or a university? It would seem a decent gesture, and you might even argue that in the long run it's smart business to reward the people on whom you depend. But maybe that is asking too much. The fact remains that if the rancher doesn't have to pay more than the going rate, he probably won't.

This shifts the question back to the cowboy. Workers in other industries have organized and demanded higher wages, fringe benefits, and profit sharing plans, and have not waited around for management to offer these benefits out of Christian charity. Why haven't cowboys done something to improve their position?

The subject of cowboy wages is a touchy one in the cattle business. I have read livestock publications for many years, but I have never seen a single article on salaries. By some unspoken agreement, it is not discussed in public. The cattle business is unique in that it is perhaps the only major industry in the United States that has never had a public airing of its labor-management problems. Or perhaps I should say that it has had only one public airing. In 1883 cowboys in the western Texas Panhandle organized to protest wages and working conditions on the LX, LS, and LIT ranches. The original ultimatum was signed by twenty-four cowboys and the strike eventually drew two hundred sympathizers. The ranches refused to bargain with the cowboys, took away their horses, cut them off the chuck line, and hired other men. In thirty days the strike was broken. As far as I can determine, this was the only time in the history of the cattle business that cowboys and ranchers showed their antagonisms to the public.

Yet the antagonisms are there. Cowboys discuss their problems with other cowboys, and ranchers discuss their problems with other ranchers, but rarely do they sit down and talk about them together, and never do they discuss them in public. In many ways this situation resembles an uneasy marriage. Neither side is entirely happy with things the way they are, but if you brought in a third party from the outside—a union organizer or a crusading journalist—cowboys and ranchers would line up together, lock arms, and send the rascal back to Chicago. Cowboys may be unhappy about wages and conditions, but they regard these matters as their own personal business, and they don't want anyone taking up their cause.

There are several explanations for this attitude, which is surely unique in the history of American labor relations. First, cowboys are so self-sufficient, independent, and isolated that nothing, except maybe a free barbecue, will bring them together for very long. The very qualities that draw a man into this solitary existence make him a poor candidate for a group or movement. He's not a joiner or a follower, and he has stoutly resisted the American way of solving problems: forming a committee. A Committee on Cowboy Problems could hold its meetings in a very small room, perhaps an outhouse or a phone booth, because nobody would show up.

Second, I think it is fair to say that cowboys do not have much of a head for business. Those who do usually put in five or ten years, starve out, and move on to another line of work in town or in the oil patch. Those who remain tend to be passive when it comes to making money. They really don't know how to make money, don't understand tax angles or complex economics, and don't have the patience or the training to sit down with a calculator and figure out how much they are worth to the operation. Consider, for example, Fay Ward's book *The Cowboy at Work,* which is probably the best and most complete manual on cowboying ever written. There is not a single entry in the index on wages, salary, or pay. The book is devoted entirely to the skills and equipment of the profession. Can you imagine a plumber's manual or a photographer's manual that did not have a section about rates and wages scales? Fay Ward cowboyed for forty years, and we must assume that during those years he did not spend much time thinking about money.

There is a third quality I have observed in cowboys that has kept them from complaining about their money problems. It is a simple, childlike trust that the boss will do what is right and fair. If the boss pays five hundred a month, the cowboy does not question it, even if he can't live on five hundred a month. He reasons that the boss is a good man, a fair man, and that he's paying all he can afford to pay. If inflation erodes the cowboy's wages, he tends to blame himself rather than the boss. "Honey," he will say to his wife when the overdrafts start coming in, "we're just spending too much money." To take up the slack, he starts breaking horses on the side or sends his wife to town to look for a job. His wife might point out that the boss had a good year and could afford to give him a raise or a bonus, but he will respond, "Honey, if the boss could afford to pay me better, I know that he would." In the last quarter of the twentieth century, when everyone seems to be out for the buck, there is something quaint and charming about this attitude, and it is a refreshing contrast to the greed of big labor unions. Unfortunately, many ranchers, past and present, have followed the natural human instinct to exploit such an attitude and have managed to use the cowboy's fundamental decency against him.

Fourth, the cowboy is in a poor bargaining position because he loves his work and because much of his labor is directed toward caring for animals, as opposed to caring for the boss or the company. He doesn't ride out in a blizzard because he wants the boss to make more money, but because there is a sick animal out there and it is the cowboy's responsibility to care for the animal, to find it, bring it home, nurse it, and keep it alive. If he thought strictly in

In spite of all the hardships involved in cowboying, young men in the modern age are still drawn to the horseback life.

terms of money, he wouldn't bother. He does it because it's right, because that's his job, and because he likes to do it.

This brings us back to a point we made earlier: cowboying is not a job, it's a way of life. The cowboy enjoys the solitude of country living, working with nature, watching the changes of the seasons, observing wildlife. He takes pride in his horsemanship and his roping. He finds satisfaction and self-expression in his work. There is only one place where he can follow this way of life: on another man's ranch. When your job is your way of life and your medium of expression, it is difficult to run a bluff on the boss, because the boss knows the truth: a cowboy would probably do it for nothing if he could get by with it.

Finally, cowboys have found it difficult to drive hard bargains with their employers because, in the end, they have more in common with ranchers than with any other class or group of people. In spite of the social differences between them, and even though they are adversaries on the matter of wages, they are cut from the same piece of leather. This is something a union organizer from the city would never comprehend, because the conventional labels and jargon of labor-versus-management, capitalist-versus-proletariat simply do not work. For all their differences, ranchers and cowboys share the same country, the same isolation, the same hardships, the same basic attitudes toward work and life. A college-educated Marxist would find tough going in ranch country. Instead of organizing a strike, he would unwittingly organize a united front of labor and management against all comers.

The economic relationship between ranchers and cowboys is complex, and it will not resolve itself into simple categories or statements. It is wrong and foolish to say that cowboys have enjoyed their poverty, but it would be just as wrong to write a crusading piece about blood-sucking ranchers. The history of the West is full of tales of shrewd landowners who exploited the basic decency of simple men and built empires out of cowboy sweat. But the cowboys allowed themselves to be exploited. They chose this way of life, they continue to choose it today, and I imagine that if there are cows to be punched in the year 2000, they will still be choosing it then.

19

The Last Cowboy?

The thesis of Jane Kramer's book *The Last Cowboy* was that the cowboy doesn't have much of a future. The frontiers have been tamed, the big pastures have been fenced, and something called agribusiness is moving into the Old West and pushing the cowboy out of the picture. Kramer is a good journalist, and she spotted the most significant trend in the modern cattle industry. She was correct in thinking that the values and goals of agribusiness are quite different from those of traditional ranching, and that the competition between the two could very well turn out to be a life-and-death struggle. However, she may have erred in ordering a coffin before there was a corpse.

The word *agribusiness,* which first appeared in farm and ranch publications in the early 1970s, means different things to different people. Some would say that it refers to the support businesses that have sprung up around agriculture, those that deal in chemicals, seeds, fertilizer, irrigation equipment, implements, and commodities. This definition might or might not include the producer (the farmer or rancher) as part of agribusiness.

My understanding of the word is more general and takes in more territory, and ultimately it points to an attitude rather than to specific industries. We can deduce this meaning from the two parts of the word: *agri* and *business.* The appearance of the word in our vocabulary marked a point in history

I think it would be a mistake to suppose that the cowboy is going to disappear anytime soon.

221

when agriculturalists began to think of agriculture more as a business than as a special calling. This change was brought about by several factors: the availability of bigger and better machinery, scientific research, and modern technology; the opening up of world markets for American farm products; and the increased sophistication of producers who were willing to incorporate new ideas and new products into their farming and ranching. But perhaps more important than any of these factors was the perception by agriculturalists that, to survive and stay in business, they would have to increase production and make use of nontraditional methods and equipment.

Agribusiness is a movement away from the way grandpa did things and toward change made possible by research and mechanization. It looks to the future, not to the past, for its models. It is moving toward the use of machines and machine energy, and away from human labor.

Jane Kramer correctly perceived that the American cowboy and his horse are standing on the railroad tracks, and that the train of agribusiness is moving toward him (though she was hardly the first to point this out). Cowboying is a profession that is bound by tradition, and the cowboy, both the working variety and the mythological shadow he has cast, is deeply rooted in the past. Whether he wants to admit it or not, he still thinks of his profession as a special calling (it certainly isn't a business), and ultimately he is part of the human labor force that agribusiness seeks to replace with machinery. To him, agribusiness means more fences, more plowed ground, more cow chutes, and more people. If he has a gut feeling that anyone involved in agribusiness doesn't have much use for a cowboy, he is probably right.

In the cattle end of the agricultural spectrum, agribusiness finds its purest form of expression in the modern feedlot, where capital investment, energy, and technology are merged in a facility which is, to put it bluntly, a beef factory. Here, vast numbers of cattle are concentrated in a small area. Their feed ration is formulated by computer, mixed by the ton in giant feed mills, and delivered to the trough by trucks. Feedlot cattle don't have to rustle for grass or seek protection from storms. They are protected from disease by antibiotics and from insects by various chemicals. All they have to do is eat, drink, and gain weight.

Feedlots are built on the typical factory model where work is highly concentrated and centralized, and skilled management is crucial. Cattlemen have discovered that they can produce finished beef more cheaply, more quickly, and more efficiently in a factory than on a ranch. The two most important components in the economic formula of a feedlot are the cost of feed grains and the cost of energy, and as long as these two components remain within a certain cost range, the factory model will work.

As a general rule, feedlots are used to finish cattle that have been born and raised on rangeland. Most steers and heifers go to the feedlot at weights ranging from six hundred to eight hundred pounds, yet the model for a totally mechanized and confined cattle industry is there in place, and under the right kind of economic conditions, the cattle business could very well proceed in this direction. It is not inconceivable that, in the years to come, we might see the entire livestock industry move toward the factory and away from the ranch. There is nothing other than the cost of energy and feed to prevent agribusinessmen from bypassing the ranch entirely as a source of stocker calves. Mother cows could be kept in a feedlot just as easily as on a ranch, and in some ways more easily, since confinement solves several management problems that exist under range conditions. Cows could be artificially inseminated and fed a ration that would stimulate their production

A feedlot cowboy riding pens and checking the condition of the cattle. If he finds sick animals, he will drive them to the "hospital" pen.

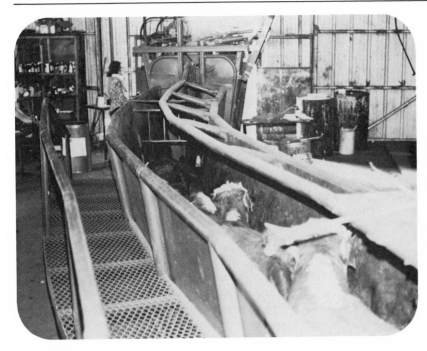

Cattle that have just arrived in a feedlot are run through this alley and held in a hydraulic squeeze chute while they are branded, marked, and vaccinated.

Doctoring sick animals is one of the daily jobs of the modern feedlot cowboy, and the work is done in a hydraulic squeeze chute.

of milk. Under this model, there would be no need for windmills, herd bulls, tenant houses—or the traditional cowboy who can ride and rope.

If trends in the cattle business move in this direction, "the last cowboy" will be an employee of a feedlot. In feedlot work, he will find regular hours and better wages than he could get on a ranch, as well as fringe benefits such as group health insurance and a pension plan. Since most feedlots are located near towns and on blacktop highways, he will probably live in town and commute to work every day, which means that he won't be stuck out on a ranch and that, after hours, he can participate in whatever social life the town has to offer. He will be working outside with animals and he will spend part of every day a-horseback. To a young man who isn't too fussy, this might appear to be the best of both worlds. He can participate in the western mystique and call himself a cowboy, but he can do it without enduring the isolation and poverty of the old-time puncher.

The feedlot cowboy is a mutant strain of the old breed. He has adapted to industrialization, and in him we can find whatever hopes or fears we feel about the future. On the positive side, we can take comfort from the fact that the cattle business in the space age still has a need for a man and a horse. On the negative side, we can hardly escape the feeling that the feedlot cowboy is only a husk of his old-time counterpart, and that much of the substance has been lost. If you are a young man who has never worked on a ranch and never known anything but feedlot work, it probably seems exciting. But if you've seen the wide-open spaces, you know what the feedlot cowboy has lost and given up.

I don't want to disparage the feedlot cowboy. He is part of the profession now, and he may be the one who carries our traditions and skills into the future. But I confess that every time I see one of them I feel a deep sadness—a sadness for him because he hasn't seen the other side, and for me because I *have* seen it, and I have loved it, and it may be passing away.

I remember one cold morning in December when I hauled a trailer load of heifers to a feedlot. I saw a cowboy on his horse, and I watched him for several minutes. He was a nice looking fellow around thirty-five years of age. He had dark hair and eyes. He looked good on his horse, and I knew he was proud to be there. He wore a nice pair of tan shotgun chaps, a black cowboy hat pulled down to his ears, a purple silk scarf tied around his neck, and a jean jacket with the collar up, and he had a cigarette hanging from the side of his mouth. He might have been a ranch cowboy in Montana, surrounded by silent pines with the snow-capped Rockies gleaming in the distance.

But he wasn't in Montana and he wasn't on a ranch. He rode his horse through acres of steel pens and looked at corpulent steers that had forgotten how to run and fight. There was no silence here, but instead the constant roar of the feed mill and the hay grinder. The mountains behind the cowboy were not the Rockies, but hills of dung that had been pushed up by front-end loaders. He sat in a new saddle, with a big dally horn wrapped with strips of rubber, a breast harness, and a roping cinch. But he carried no rope. Neither did the other men on the crew. And I thought to myself: "Well, cowboy, they've taken away your rope. Tomorrow, they'll take away your horse and issue you a Honda motorcycle. Horseman, pass by."

Those of us who have known the past and have helped to shape it have a tendency to view the future with suspicion and fear, and to view change in terms of apocolypse. That is often a mistake. Things change and life goes on. Agribusiness is moving us toward an agriculture in which cowboys are replaced by technology, but the Achilles' heel of agribusiness is its reliance upon petroleum energy—not only the electricity which runs the feed mill

A young cowboy buckles up his chaps and gets ready to hit the saddle. Even in the age of space travel and computers, the horseback life continues to lure a few hardy young men.

and the diesel fuel which runs the trucks, but also the feed grains that are the basic commodity in the feeding industry. Corn and milo, raised on irrigated farms, are not merely the harvest of benevolent Nature; they are petroleum energy (tractor fuel, irrigation fuel, herbicide, and fertilizer) that has been translated into organic material. Given the volatile state of energy markets in 1980, it is entirely possible that trends in the cattle business which began around 1960 will change, and that skyrocketing energy costs will force the industry to return to methods which require less energy, less technology, and less machinery. This trend could see fewer cattle moving into feedlots and more cattle going back to the ranches. By raising the price of our oil, the OPEC nations might be changing our taste in beef, from grain-fed to grass-fed.

But regardless of what happens in the feeding industry, I think it would be a mistake to suppose that the cowboy is going to disappear anytime soon. This country has millions of acres of rangeland that will never be suitable for farming or urban development or anything but pasturing livestock. And where you find a pasture and a herd of cows, you will find a cowboy riding through them on his horse. The cowboy will survive, because there is still no machine or combination of machines that can do the job better than a good man on a good horse; and because the mystique and challenge of cowboying will continue to draw young men into the profession.

20

Books about Cowboys

The little man in high heel boots has cast a very large shadow across our land.

The golden age of writing about the cowboy occurred in the years from about 1920 to 1955. During this period the best writers and writing we have on the subject of the old-time cowboy emerged, and the authors of this period have now become the leading authorities on the subject. It appears to me that modern writers have a tendency to believe, first, that "real" cowboys disappeared years ago and that those who remain are hardly worth discussing; and, second, that writers of J. Frank Dobie's generation exhausted the subject and said everything that needed saying. This has produced a kind of inbred literature in which modern writers warm up and rearrange the old verities, often quoting Dobie and Andy Adams and Philip Ashton Rollins without knowing it, or at least without acknowledging it. Dobie made western writing respectable and blazed the trail for regional writers who followed. He so thoroughly dominated the field that, today, when we want to know something about cowboys, we have a tendency to repeat his observations instead of looking around for our own.

There are two problems with this approach. The first is that times have changed a great deal since Dobie was collecting cowboy stories from the old trail drivers, and cowboying has changed with the times. The second is that Dobie was not as interested in cowboys as one might suppose. The three books which critics have singled out as his best, *The Longhorns, The Mustangs,* and *Tongues of the Monte,* were not about cowboys at all, or dealt with the subject only in passing. His best book about cowboying was his first, *A Vaquero of the Brush Country,* which contains excellent material about cow work in the brush country of South Texas. Dobie's part in the writing of this book was rather odd. The ''I'' in the narrative is not Dobie, even though he is listed as the author, but rather a man named John Young. Young told the stories and supplied the details; Dobie polished up the prose and added background material. Dobie must be given the credit for discovering John Young and getting the book published, but the real strength of the work lies in Young's knowledge of the cowboy profession.

Dobie did not write exclusively about cowboys, and in fact he appears to have been more interested in horses, longhorn cattle, Texas wildlife, treasure stories, and western literature. Cowboys fascinated him, but so did many other things. Nor was he as much an authority on cowboying as many readers have supposed, because he himself was not one. He grew up on a ranch in Live Oak County, Texas. As a young man he worked cattle and rode horseback. He knew vaqueros and saw them in action, and for a time he even managed a ranch for his uncle Jim Dobie. But he was not, strictly speaking, a cowboy, meaning a man who is paid wages for his ability to ride, rope, and endure hardship. I doubt that he had the skills or instincts to have made his living as a cowboy (toward the end of his life he admitted that he was never a good rider or roper), and he certainly did not have the temperament of one. His active mind and free spirit would have made him miserable as a wage-earning cowhand. And if he fulminated against the low salary he received at the University of Texas (he had no Ph.D. and seemed doomed to untenured penury), he would have found cowboy wages intolerable.

To say that Dobie was never a cowboy is not to say that he was ignorant on the subject or had no right to record cowboy lore, but to make a more important point, which is that his view of the cowboy tended to be abstract and romantic. In his introduction to *A Vaquero of the Brush Country,* he wrote:

> No genuine cowboy ever suffered from an inferiority complex or ranked himself in the "laboring class." . . . He considered himself a *cavalier* in the full sense of that word—a gentleman on horse, privileged to come it proud over all . . . earth-clinging creatures. . . . He was the aristocrat of all wage earners. . . . The ranch owner was a kind of feudal lord over his range principality, but he made no attempt to lord it over his Anglo-American cowboys. [P. xii]

That sounds good, good enough so that two generations of readers and scholars have picked up Dobie's ideas and have repeated them. But these were merely his opinions, and his opinions on cowboying were not as accurate as his views on other subjects. Any man who has ever worked twelve and fourteen hour days for cowboy wages cannot help being puzzled by Dobie's windy pronouncement that "no genuine cowboy ever . . . ranked himself in the laboring class."

It is significant that in describing the cowboy, Dobie used terms drawn from the age of chivalry: cowboy as cavalier or knight, and rancher as feudal lord. As a boy in the harsh South Texas brush country, Dobie nourished his imagination on the romantic literature of Scott and Tennyson. "I was a knight in the image of Ivanhoe and with my brother Elrich set up a tournament course. . . . Tennyson's *Idylls of the King* put me into a world where for months wan lights flickered on the plains farther away than Troy" (*Some*

Styles and equipment have changed over the years, but the cowboy's fascination with his catch rope is as strong today as it was a hundred years ago. A good man, mounted on a good horse and holding a nice little loop in his hands, is still the best cow-tending machine in the world.

Part of Myself, pp. 16, 17). Ranchers in South Texas were indeed "feudal lords," but young Dobie never saw the back side of the feudal system because he was the son of a rancher-lord, and because he was able to soften the harsher qualities of the system through the filter of romantic literature. Hence, he could say, and believe, that the cowboy was a cavalier, a gentleman on horseback, and the aristocrat of all wage earners, and that the rancher was a benevolent lord who treated his knights with respect and kindness.

Dobie's view of cowboys was conditioned by his place in the social system. He saw them from the perspective of a rancher, so that they were always *them* instead of *us, him* instead of *me.* The qualities he admired in the cowboy were those of a good knight or vassal: "a proud rider . . . unyielding, daring, punctilious in a code peculiar to his occupation, and faithful to his trust" (*Vaquero,* p. xii). The cowboy's "trust" was taking care of someone else's property, for which he was expected to sacrifice comfort, health, and even his life. Dobie admired this kind of loyalty in the cowboy, as would any rancher or rancher's son.

What Dobie observed in the cowboy was not false or wholly incorrect; the heroism, the virtue, the nobility were there. But there was more to the cowboy, and Dobie tended to gloss over it. You get the feeling that he chose to keep his emotional distance from the cowboy and to leave him partially shrouded in the romantic past.

In their fine book *The American Cowboy: The Myth and The Reality,* Joe B. Frantz and Julian Ernest Choate say that, "passing by Dobie . . . the most notable of the truthtellers is undoubtedly J. Evetts Haley . . . " (pp. 188–90). I can understand their admiration for Mr. Dobie, but there is no question in my mind that, of the two men, Haley was far more knowledgeable about cowboys and cowboying. Both men came from range backgrounds, both chose to go into scholarship, and both ended up on the faculty of the University of Texas. But where Dobie drifted away from his association with the working cowboy, toward folklore, literature, and his public career as ''Mr. Texas,'' Haley burrowed deeper and deeper into the Texas soil. He answered the call of the wild by going to the wilderness: he moved to the Panhandle, set up shop in Canyon, and started writing excellent books about range history. At the same time, he also immersed himself in operating his JH Ranch, south of Spearman, and kept in touch with ''the problems of life as derived from grass'' (*Life on the Texas Range: Photographs by Erwin E. Smith,* p. 29).

Because Haley kept his hand in the cattle business, his descriptions of ranch work were accurate and to the point. He wrote with the easy confidence of a man who knew the cowboy profession from the inside, and you sense that his instincts were the same as those of the people he wrote about. Consider this passage from his masterwork, *Charles Goodnight, Cowman and Plainsman:* ''This particular morning Mitchell took a circle for the horses and met a nice black bear. To expect him to pass up such a chance was like expecting a hungry cow to pass up a beargrass bloom. Frank jerked down his rope, shook out a little loop, and took after the bear . . .'' (p. 407).

The metaphor of the cow passing up a beargrass bloom is perfectly drawn, and it tells us as much about Haley as it does about Frank Mitchell, the cowboy. It tells us that Haley had experienced the frustration of trying to drive cattle across the prairie country in the spring, when every cow in the bunch wanted to pause and eat the tender white blooms of the beargrass plant. His description of the roping process is brief and unadorned, and spoken just exactly as a working cowboy would have said it: ''Frank *jerked down* his rope, *shook out* a little loop, and *took after* the bear.''

Philip Ashton Rollins's *The Cowboy: An Unconventional History of Civilization on the Old-Time Cattle Range* was originally published in 1922 and reissued as a paperback in 1979. It is a comprehensive work about the old-time cowboy, covering all phases of his life and work. Rollins was a scholar who had spent time ''upon the open Range'' in Wyoming near the end of the nineteenth century, and he described in detail the cowboy's equipment, routine, tools, social life, and working environment. It's unfortunate that he wrote such congested prose. The book is hard to read. By the time you reach the end of one of his Teutonic sentences, you have forgotten what he said at the beginning. But *The Cowboy* is an excellent reference book and contains a wealth of information about the nineteenth-century cowboy.

Fay Ward's *The Cowboy at Work: All About His Job and How He Does It* is perhaps the best book ever written about the working cowboy. Ward spent forty years working on ranches from Canada to Mexico, and his book is so complete in detail and so simply written that you can actually use it as a training manual. There is no pretension in his writing. He isn't a scholar and doesn't want to be one. Nor does he try to impress the reader that he was a rough, tough, shoot-'em-up cowboy. Consider, for example, his very sensible remarks on horse-breaking:

''Bronc-fighter'' is a term that should be used only to designate those bronc riders who do a horse more harm than good. . . . The methods for handlin' broncs described in the following pages are based on the principle that the horse deserves humane treatment and that there should be due regard for the safety of the rider. . . . Time, patience, kindness, and system are the main factors for breaking horses successfully for whatever purpose. [P. 107]

I have an idea that Fay Ward was always well mounted, because he understood that breaking a horse is not the same as conquering him, and that horse breaking is a method of teaching the animal to do what you want him to do.

Ward's chapter on ropes and roping is unsurpassed in the literature of the cowboy. In thirty pages he describes what a rope is, what it can do, and how the old-time cowboy went about using it. He describes roping techniques in simple language and illustrates the text with his own drawings, which are extremely well done.

I doubt that anyone will ever learn the cowboy trade by reading a book, but if you wanted to give it a try, Fay Ward's book would be the place to start.

Ben K. Green is another of my favorite cowboy writers, though his approach was quite different from Ward's. Whereas Ward set out to write a manual on cowboying, Green was more interested in telling yarns, and in the process of telling them, he revealed a tremendous store of knowledge about horses, cattle, and roping. I have always been surprised at the success of Ben Green's books—and they have been very successful; in 1979 Knopf brought out its twelfth printing of *Wild Cow Tales*—because he was not a good writer. He was not even a particularly friendly writer. You get the impression that he was indifferent to people and that when he told a story, he was not much interested in whether the reader was listening or not. Readers usually sense this kind of attitude in an author and resent it. Somehow Ben Green got by with it, and his books continue to sell. I think the secret to his success as a writer was that he had something to say, and he said it in his own natural voice.

He wrote with a kind of don't-give-a-damn attitude that was irreverent, refreshing, and funny. Many readers take this as a sign of honesty in the man. Perhaps it is, but I have grown a little suspicious of old Doc and have wondered if he really did all the things he claimed to have done. If you read Ben Green and Fay Ward back-to-back, you will discover that many of the techniques Green used on wild cattle and horses, and which he attributed to his own cleverness, were known and widely used by cowboys of the time. Ward makes that clear, while Green leaves you with the impression that he invented them himself. It has also troubled me that you can read *A Thousand Miles of Mustangin'* and *Wild Cow Tales,* both of which describe Green's use of the rope, and you will never find one mention of a missed loop. I don't doubt that Ben Green was an excellent roper. But no matter how good you are, a certain percentage of your throws are going to miss the mark when the calf turns the wrong way, the horse doesn't give you good position, the wind causes the loop to float, or you have to hurry your throw. The result is a miss. Cowboys don't like to talk about their misses, especially when they come two or three in a row, but that's part of the game. Cowboys know that and accept it. Ben Green knew it too, but he kept mum about it. It makes me wonder if there were other things he didn't bother to mention.

But of course it really doesn't matter whether he was the best or worst roper who ever lived. He wrote delightful books, which is something most ropers can't do, and anyone who reads them will absorb a great deal of information about cowboying during the period from 1925 to 1940.

Old Doc has passed on to his eternal reward and will write no more, but we have another writer around who is mining the same rich seam of ore. His name is Spike Van Cleve. He operates a ranch near Big Timber, Montana, and he wrote a delightful book called *40 Years' Gatherin's.* He introduces himself to the reader with these words:

I am a lucky man. I was born, grew up, and have lived all my life in what I figure is the prettiest country God ever made—under the Crazy Mountains at the western edge of the high plains of south central Montana. [P. xiii]
I am a horse man. I was raised with them, have lived with them all my life, and I hope I'll die with them. [P. 83]

But Spike is more than a lucky man and a man of the horse. He is a man who sees and feels deeply, who belongs to a place, and who writes well enough to share his world with others. Through his eyes and ears, the reader is able to experience the savage delight of being a cowboy in a wild country. Spike has an ear for dialect and the nuances of language, and an outrageous sense of humor that you could only describe as pure cowboy—or, to use one of his own expressions, "pure quill." Anyone who can read *40 Years' Gatherin's* without bursting into laughter a dozen times should visit an undertaker.

I don't consider myself an authority on cowboy fiction, but I like the way novelist Elmer Kelton handles the subject. He understands cowboys and knows them to the core, and over the years he has maintained a close association with the cattle business as a writer for the *Livestock Weekly,* which is probably the best cow paper published in America today. *The Time It Never Rained* is a fine book (it won both the Spur and Western Heritage awards), but I think *The Good Old Boys* is even better. This is not just a shoot-'em-up or a genre western, but a thoughtful novel that probes themes that run deep in the western mind.

The story centers upon Hewey Calloway, a cowboy who is caught in a struggle between his desire to marry and settle down and the lure of cowboy freedom. To his credit, Kelton does not make the choice an easy or a simple one. He understands the raw power of the Old West and the freedom of the nomadic cowboy, but he also understands the cost of it. *The Good Old Boys* deals with the conflict between old and new, between romance and civilization, between freedom and whatever it is that has replaced it in our modern world. Kelton does not attempt to resolve this conflict or to provide a simple solution.

In 1977 a New York-based journalist named Jane Kramer published a book called *The Last Cowboy.* It received good reviews in the eastern press and was heralded as an important work on the modern cowboy. I read it and was disappointed.

It is a peculiar book. On the one hand Kramer appears to be writing nonfiction. The book is set on a modern-day ranch in the Texas Panhandle. She uses the names of towns in the area. In chapters five and seven she does an excellent job of explaining the development of the cattle business, from the trail drives of old to the modern feedyard. It's good stuff. Obviously Kramer knows how to research a story.

Yet the rest of the book gives the appearance of being a novel, the kind that searches for meaning. And the meaning the "serious" novel often finds is that the main character is a failure—a "failed" author, a "failed" advertising executive, and so forth. When Kramer tells us in her introduction that Henry Blanton's story is "a kind of parable of failed promise" (p. ix), we get the first hint of what's coming: a book which seems to be a nonfiction account of a Texas cowboy, but which is actually a novel about another American failure. But this failure is something special because cowboys are something special. The cowboy, after all, is an American myth or archetype. If the cowboy is failed, then the myth is failed. Kramer's book is an eschatological novel. She is brooding over lost things and the end of something.

Kramer pushes too hard to wring meaning out of the archetypal cowboy, and her major character, Henry Blanton, is not made of archetypal stuff. When she gives us Henry Blanton, sitting on his grandfather's chuck wagon out in the yard, "mourning the West that was supposed to be," remembering his favorite Hollywood heroes, and drinking whiskey, he looks like a fool. The poor man has been sent to the literary taxidermist, stuffed, and put on display as a national symbol of "failed promise."

I wish that Kramer had settled on writing either a novel or a work of nonfiction—in other words, that she had either written what she *thought* or what she *observed*. Instead, she tried to combine them in one form and to impose the eastern intellectual community's sense of failure upon a western landscape. The result is a book that seems, in spots, contrived and pushy. The fact is that Henry Blanton is *not* the last cowboy, and he may not even be the next-to-the-last.

What Kramer attempted to do in *The Last Cowboy,* Larry McMurtry succeeded in doing in his book of essays *In a Narrow Grave.* McMurtry shares Kramer's view that the cowboy, both the physical being and the archetype, is riding off into a sunset from which he will never return. The major difference between them is that McMurtry, who was raised on a ranch in Archer County, Texas, and who comes from an old and respected ranching family, is able to comprehend and express such an event. He writes,

Living (in Texas) consciously uses a great deal of one's blood: it involves one at once in a birth, a death, and a bitter love affair. . . . The death . . . moves me—the way of life that is dying had its value. Its appeal was simple, but genuine, and it called to it and is taking with it people whom one could not but love. . . . The place where all my stories start is the heart faced suddenly with the loss of its country, its customary and legendary range. [PP. xv, 140]

One of McMurtry's stories was a novel called *Horseman, Pass By,* which was made into the movie *Hud.* Hud Bannon, a young rancher-cowboy, "is one of the many people whose capacities no longer fit their situations. He needs more room and less company, and is unlikely to get either" (p. 27). In McMurtry's view, Hud represents the modern cowboy who is fenced out of his old range, whose mythological roots are dying, and who responds with rage and violence. C. L. Sonnichsen takes a less charitable view of Hud, calling him "a complete SOB " and saying that he "brings seventy years of doubt about the cowboy hero to final disillusion" *(From Hopalong to Hud: Thoughts on Western Fiction).*

Regardless of what you think of Hud Bannon, McMurtry's book of essays is brilliant and provocative and will endure in the literature of the cowboy. In *Narrow Grave* you don't learn much about the working cowboy or what he does in the course of a day. McMurtry is not painting realistic pictures of windmills, Hereford cows, or life on the range. He is interested in the head-on collision of old and new, in which the cowboy and everything he represents is splattered by the freight train of modern change. In one breath McMurtry expresses his grief and carefully measures his sense of loss. In the next breath we hear him laughing like a demon and saying, "Good riddance!" McMurtry seems capable of criticizing everything around him, and many readers have been outraged by his lack of respect for convention and tradition. But the paradox we find in his essays is not original with him, and he did not create it from nothing. The paradox is present in our society. We are a people who claim to revere the heroic ideals of the cowboy, yet we have built a way of life that is driving him to the wall. McMurtry has the annoying habit of calling attention to such things.

No matter which version of the cowboy you prefer—the action-humor version, the historical, the factual, the fictional, or the eschatological—there is one point on which we should all agree: the little man in high heel boots has cast a very large shadow across our land. No one can say whether he will ride with us into the twenty-first century or turn his horse and lope back into the past. But I have a feeling that, in one form or another, he will be with us as long as there is a place called America, and that we will continue to find him in our dreams and in our deepest vision of ourselves.

Bibliography

Dobie, J. Frank. *Cow People*. Boston: Little, Brown and Co., 1964.

———. *The Longhorns*. Boston: Little, Brown and Co., 1941.

———. *On The Open Range*. Dallas: Banks, Upshaw and Co., 1931.

———. *Some Part of Myself*. Boston: Little, Brown and Co., 1967.

———. *A Vaquero of the Brush Country*. Dallas: Southwest Press, 1929.

Erickson, John R. *Panhandle Cowboy*. Lincoln: University of Nebraska Press, 1980.

———. "Pasture Roping over the Years, Part 1." *Cattleman Magazine*, October 1979, pp. 48–56.

———. "Pasture Roping over the Years, Part 2." *Cattleman Magazine*, November 1979, pp. 100–102, 106–108.

Frantz, Joe B., and Choate, Julian Ernest. *The American Cowboy: The Myth and the Reality*. Norman: University of Oklahoma Press, 1955.

Green, Ben K. *A Thousand Miles of Mustangin'*. Flagstaff: Northland Press, 1972.

———. *Wild Cow Tales*. New York: Alfred A. Knopf, 1969.

Haley, J. Evetts. *Charles Goodnight, Cowman and Plainsman*. Boston and New York: Houghton Mifflin Co., 1936.

———. *George W. Littlefield, Texan*. Norman: University of Oklahoma Press, 1943.

———. *Life on the Texas Range: Photographs by Erwin E. Smith*. Austin: University of Texas Press, 1973.

———. *The XIT Ranch of Texas*. Norman: University of Oklahoma Press, New edition, 1953.

Kelton, Elmer. *The Good Old Boys*. New York: Doubleday and Co., 1978.

———. *The Time It Never Rained*. New York: Ace Books, 1973.

Kramer, Jane. *The Last Cowboy*. New York: Harper and Row, 1977.

McMurtry, Larry. *Horseman, Pass By*. New York: Harper and Row, 1961.

———. *In a Narrow Grave: Essays on Texas*. Austin: Encino Press, 1968.

Mora, Jo. *Trail Dust and Saddle Leather*. New York: Scribner's, 1946.

Perkins, Peter. *Cowboys of the High Sierra*. Flagstaff: Northland Press, 1980.

Rollins, Philip Ashton. *The Cowboy: An Unconventional*

History of Civilization on the Old-time Cattle Range. Albuquerque: University of New Mexico Press, 1979.

Sonnichsen, C. L. *From Hopalong to Hud: Thoughts on Western Fiction.* College Station: Texas A&M Press, 1978.

Van Cleve, Spike. *40 Years' Gatherin's.* Kansas City: Lowell Press, 1977.

Ward, Fay E. *The Cowboy at Work: All About His Job and How He Does It.* New York: Hastings House Publishers, 1958.

Acknowledgments

Before I quit this book, I would like to acknowledge and thank the men who taught me most of what I know about cowboying: Gordon Wright, Henry Hale, Lawrence Ellzey, Tom Ellzey, Mark Mayo, Sandy Hagar, Stanley Barby, Jake Parker, Pat Mason, and Glen Green.

I am indebted to Myron McCartor for reading the manuscript and making suggestions on ways to improve it. My thanks also to Joseph Erickson, Don Worcester, Paul Boller, Jeanne Williams, Elmer Kelton, and Marc Simmons for the encouragement they have given me over the years.

And my deepest thanks go to Kris, my bride of thirteen years, who did the photography for this book. She has accompanied me to some strange places and has blessed me with her love.